THREADS

from the

'30s

QUILTS USING
REPRODUCTION FABRICS

Compiled by
Nancy J. Martin

Martingale
& C O M P A N Y

CREDITS

President . . . . Nancy J. Martin
CEO/Publisher . . . . Daniel J. Martin
Associate Publisher . . . . Jane Hamada
Editorial Director . . . . Mary V. Green
Technical Editor . . . . Darra Williamson
Copy Editor . . . . Ellen Balstad
Illustrator . . . . Laurel Strand
Photographer . . . . Brent Kane
Designer . . . . Rohani Design

That Patchwork Place is an imprint of
Martingale & Company.

Mission Statement
We are dedicated to providing quality products
and service by working together to inspire creativity
and to enrich the lives we touch.

Threads from the '30s: Quilts Using Reproduction
Fabrics
© 2000 by Martingale & Company

Martingale & Company
20205 144th Avenue NE
Woodinville, WA 98072-8478 USA
www.martingale-pub.com

Printed in China
07 06 05 04 03 02 01   10 9 8 7 6 5 4

Library of Congress Cataloging-in-Publication Data

Threads from the '30 : quilts using reproduction
    fabrics / compiled by Nancy J. Martin.
        p. cm.
    ISBN 1-56477-314-0
    1. Patchwork—Patterns. 2. Patchwork quilts—
United States—History—20th century. 3. Textile
fabrics—Reproduction. I. Title: Threads from the
thirties. II. Martin, Nancy J.

TT835 .T484 2000
746.46'041—dc21

99-089520

CONTENTS

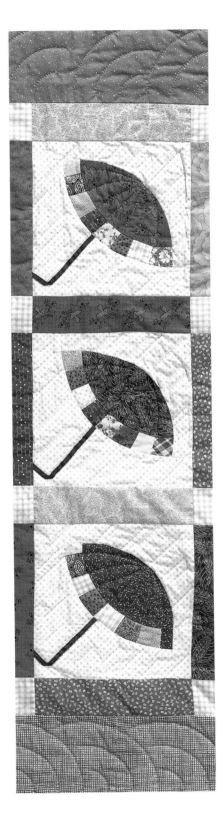

INTRODUCTION

While on a recent tour of local quilt shops, I was amazed to see the wide selection of '30s reproduction prints. Walking into a room full of these sunny, happy colors made me want to hurry home and begin stitching. I wondered what types of quilts these '30s reproduction prints were being used for, and I asked the shop owners. Their response was that very few books exist that show a quilter how to use these popular patterns and prints. I immediately thought of talented quilt designers I know who could contribute to a book based on reproduction '30s fabrics. Within days I contacted the contributors for this book and was gratified by their positive response. I knew that they would enjoy the challenge of working with reproduction fabrics. I also felt that they would capture the essence of '30s quilts but employ up-to-date construction techniques. I hope their quilts will serve as an inspiration as you stitch your "threads from the '30s."

Nancy J. Martin

HISTORY OF 1930s FABRICS

World events and trends in society all shaped the 1930s, when a quilting revival was reaching its peak. This quilt revival started as early as the 1920s, when a return to classic architecture with clean-cut lines, colonial homes, Cape Cod cottages, and bungalows with simple, unpretentious furnishings became popular. Collecting antiques was fashionable. This, in turn, caused an increased interest in patchwork quilts, which suited the colonial and Cape Cod decor. Women bought yardage specifically for these quilts rather than create scrap bag versions.

After World War I, German dyes were once again available, and fabrics blossomed in cheery prints. Various advances in printing had also been made, so that a wide range of colors was available and almost any pattern could be printed. Quilters indulged in watermelon pinks, mint greens, and lemon yellows. They turned away from the fabrics used earlier in the century, which reflected a darker palette and tiny traditional motifs.

In addition to the colorful fabrics, quilts with juvenile themes for young children emerged. These nursery themes were often available in commercial kits that featured characters such as Raggedy Ann and Andy, the Three Bears, toy soldiers, dolls, the alphabet, Sunbonnet girls, and even a marionette show. These designs marked the realization that the young child was not a miniature adult but had a unique personality with distinct interests. Crib quilts were no longer miniature versions of quilts enjoyed by adults. The new designs were scaled for, and intended to be used in, children's quilts.

As the 1930s began, other influences started to appear in fabric design. Art movements like cubism and surrealism were catching the imagination of designers, but soon the Depression began to affect everyone. Manufacturers cut cost by lowering the thread count of fabric. Many patterns were printed in one color on white, or space was left around each color so no care had to be taken with the registration of the design.

During this period, newspapers helped spread the growth of quilting with their regular quilting columns. The *Kansas City Star*, which published editions in Missouri, Kansas, Arkansas, and Oklahoma—the heartland of quilting—was the most famous of these. Printed quilt patterns were featured on a weekly basis, beginning in September 1928. Avid quilters collected these columns, often pasting them in notebooks and composition books. Many quilt patterns were ordered by mail from other newspaper columns.

Sara Nephew, in her book *My Mother's Quilts: Designs from the Thirties*, comments that "quilting has often been a consolation to ladies with difficult lives, and the '30s were difficult. These women must have looked forward to the weekly quilt patterns in the newspaper, digging through their feedsack bags of fabric scraps and planning something beautiful, when they found a pattern they especially liked."[1]

Thomas K. Woodard, quilt historian, in his book *Twentieth Century Quilts 1900–1950*, states that "quilting also satisfied a deep need to be thrifty and industrious, two age-old American virtues especially valued during the Depression."[2] Woodard also says that quilting satisfied another "very deep need in America—a need to tap into a tradition of handiwork that was vanishing from women's lives as their homes became more automated with the sewing machine, the automatic washer, the vacuum cleaner, and other high-tech trappings of modernity. Particularly during the Depression, quilting gave women a profound sense of accomplishment, of being able to *do* something at a time when the labor force was idle and to *piece* something together when people's lives were falling apart."[3]

In our present high-tech era of computers, remote controls, and automated technology, cheery '30s prints fill our need for nostalgia and a return to simpler times. It's satisfying to make a quilt with '30s reproduction fabrics and reflect on what was in the minds of our quilting sisters of yesteryear as they used these same fabrics.

Notes
   1. Sara Nephew, *My Mother's Quilts: Designs from the Thirties* (Bothell, Wash.: That Patchwork Place, 1988).
   2. Thos. K. Woodard and Blanche Greenstein, *Twentieth Century Quilts 1900–1950* (New York: E. P. Dutton, 1988).
   3. Ibid.

QUILTMAKING BASICS

◆ Fabric

Select high-quality, 100 percent cotton fabrics. They hold their shape well and are easy to handle. Cotton blends can be more difficult to stitch and press. Sometimes, however, a cotton blend is worth a little extra effort if it is the perfect fabric for your quilt.

Yardage requirements are provided for all the projects in this book and are based on 42" of usable fabric after prewashing. A wide variety of wonderful 1930s-style reproduction fabrics is available today, making it easy and exciting to re-create the distinctive look of the '30s quilt. If you are lucky enough to have access to vintage fabrics, mix them freely with these charming reproduction pieces and other similarly tinted fabrics from your stash.

Some quilts call for an assortment of scraps, or can easily be adapted for the scrappy look. If you have a collection of scraps, feel free to use them and purchase only those fabrics you need to complete the quilt you are making.

Prewash all fabrics to test for colorfastness and to remove excess dye. Wash dark and light colors separately so that dark colors do not run onto light fabrics. Some fabrics may require several rinses to eliminate the excess dyes. Iron the fabrics so that you can cut out the pieces accurately.

◆ Supplies

Sewing Machine: To machine piece, you'll need a sewing machine that has a good straight stitch. You'll also need a walking foot or darning foot if you are going to machine quilt.

Rotary-Cutting Tools: You will need a rotary cutter, cutting mat, and clear acrylic rulers in a variety of sizes, such as 6" × 24" and 12" × 12". A Bias Square® ruler is helpful for trimming half-square triangles and other square units, and for straightening the edges of fabric for rotary cutting.

Thread: Use a good-quality, all-purpose cotton or cotton-covered polyester thread.

Needles: For machine piecing, a size 10/70 or 12/80 works well for most cottons. For hand appliqué, choose a needle that will glide easily through the edges of the appliqué pieces. Size 10 (fine) to size 12 (very fine) needles work well.

Pins: Long, fine "quilters' pins" with glass or plastic heads are easy to handle. Small ½"- to ¾"-long sequin pins work well for appliqué.

Sandpaper Board: This is an invaluable tool for accurately marking fabric. You can easily make one by adhering very fine sandpaper to a hard surface, such as wood, cardboard, poster board, or needlework mounting board. The sandpaper grabs the fabric and keeps it from slipping as you mark.

Scissors: Use your best scissors to cut only fabric. Use an older pair of scissors to cut paper, cardboard, and template plastic. Small 4" scissors with sharp points are handy for clipping thread.

Template Plastic: Use clear or frosted plastic (available at quilt shops) to make durable, accurate templates.

Seam Ripper: Use this tool to remove stitches from incorrectly sewn seams.

Marking Tools: A variety of tools are available to mark fabric when tracing around templates or for marking quilting designs. Use a sharp #2 pencil or fine-lead mechanical pencil on lighter-colored fabrics, and a silver or yellow marking pencil on darker fabrics. Chalk pencils or chalk-wheel markers also make clear marks on fabric. *Be sure to test your marking tool to make sure you can remove the marks easily.*

◆ Rotary Cutting

Instructions for quick-and-easy rotary cutting are provided wherever possible. All measurements include standard $\frac{1}{4}$"-wide seam allowances. For those unfamiliar with rotary cutting, a brief introduction is provided below. For more detailed information, see *Shortcuts: A Concise Guide to Rotary Cutting* by Donna Lynn Thomas (Martingale & Company, 1999).

1. Fold the fabric and match selvages, aligning the crosswise and lengthwise grains as much as possible. Place the folded edge closest to you on the cutting mat. Align a square ruler such as a Bias Square along the folded edge of the fabric. Place a long, straight ruler to the left of the square ruler, just covering the uneven raw edges of the left side of the fabric.

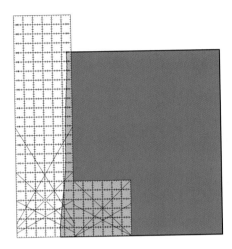

Remove the square ruler and cut along the right edge of the long ruler, rolling the rotary cutter away from you. Discard this strip. (Reverse this procedure if you are left-handed.)

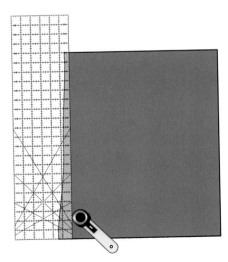

2. To cut strips, align the newly cut edge of the fabric with the ruler markings at the required width. For example, to cut a 3"-wide strip, place the 3" ruler mark on the edge of the fabric.

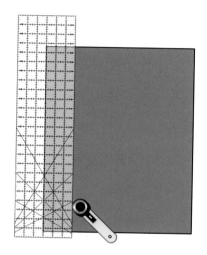

3. To cut squares, cut strips in the required widths. Trim the selvage ends of the strips. Align the left edge of the strips with the correct ruler markings. The sides of each square should have the same measurement as the width of the strips. Cut the strips into squares. Continue cutting squares until you have the number needed.

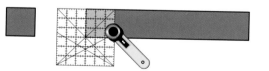

4. To make a half-square triangle, first cut a square. Cut the square ⅞" larger than the finished size of the *short* side of the triangle; then cut the square once diagonally, corner to corner. Each square yields 2 half-square triangles. The short sides of each triangle are on the straight grain of the fabric.

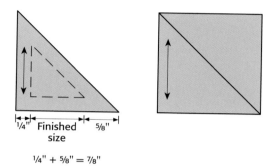

¼" Finished size ⅝"

¼" + ⅝" = ⅞"

5. To make a quarter-square triangle, first cut a square. Cut the square 1¼" larger than the finished size of the *long* edge of the triangle; then cut the square twice diagonally, corner to corner. Each square yields 4 quarter-square triangles. The long side of each triangle is on the straight grain of the fabric.

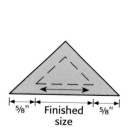
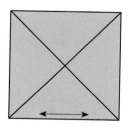

⅝" Finished size ⅝"

⅝" + ⅝" = 1¼"

◆ Machine Piecing

Most blocks in this book are designed for easy rotary cutting and quick piecing. Some blocks, however, require the use of templates for particular shapes, such as "Summer in Seattle" on page 58. Templates for machine piecing include the required $\frac{1}{4}$"-wide seam allowances. Cut out the templates on the outside lines so that they include the seam allowances. Be sure to mark the pattern name and grain-line arrow on each template.

The most important thing to remember about machine piecing is to maintain a consistent $\frac{1}{4}$"-wide seam allowance. Otherwise, the quilt blocks will not be the desired finished size. If that happens, the size of everything else in the quilt is affected, including alternate blocks, sashings, and borders. Measurements for all components of each quilt are based on blocks that finish accurately to the desired size plus $\frac{1}{4}$" on each edge for seam allowances.

Take the time to establish an exact $\frac{1}{4}$"-wide seam guide on your machine. Some machines have a special quilting foot that measures exactly $\frac{1}{4}$" from the center needle position to the edge of the foot. This feature allows you to use the edge of the presser foot to guide the fabric for a perfect $\frac{1}{4}$"-wide seam allowance.

If your machine doesn't have such a foot, create a seam guide by placing the edge of a piece of tape, moleskin, or a magnetic seam guide $\frac{1}{4}$" away from the needle.

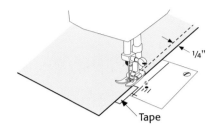

Tape

Chain Piecing

Chain piecing is an efficient system that saves time and thread. The following steps describe the process.

1. Sew the first pair of pieces from cut edge to cut edge, using 12–15 stitches per inch. At the end of the seam, stop sewing but *do not* cut the thread.

2. Feed the next pair of pieces under the presser foot, as close as possible to the first. Continue feeding pieces through the machine without cutting the threads in between the pairs.

3. When all the pieces are sewn, remove the chain from the machine and clip the threads between the pairs of sewn pieces.

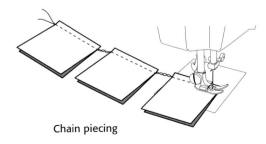

Chain piecing

Easing

If two pieces being sewn together are slightly different in size (less than ⅛"), pin the places where the two pieces should match, and in between if necessary, to distribute the excess fabric evenly. Sew the seam with the longer piece on the bottom. The feed dogs will ease the two pieces together.

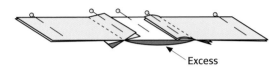

Excess

Pressing

The traditional rule in quiltmaking is to press seams to one side, toward the darker color wherever possible. First press the seams flat from the back side of the fabric; then press the seams in the desired direction from the front side. Press carefully to avoid distorting the shapes.

When joining two seamed units, plan ahead and press the seam allowances in opposite directions as shown. This reduces bulk and makes it easier to match the seam lines. The seam allowances will butt against each other where two seams meet, making it easier to join units with perfectly matched seam intersections.

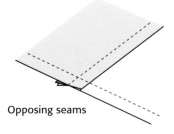

Opposing seams

Cut-and-Pieced Squares

This quick-piecing method works well when you need only a small number of half-square triangle units, or when you need units in several different combinations (see "Barney and Friends" on page 66). It requires careful pressing after the squares are stitched and cut to avoid distorting the finished units.

1. Cut squares the size instructed in the project directions for the quilt. Pair squares as directed in the instructions, right sides together.

2. Draw a diagonal line from corner to corner on the back of the lightest fabric.

3. Sew ¼" from the drawn line on both sides.

4. Cut on the drawn line. Carefully press the seams toward the darker fabric and trim the "dog-ear"corners. Each pair of squares you sew together yields 2 half-square triangle units.

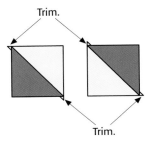

Trim.

Trim.

Basic Appliqué

General instructions are provided here for the three different appliqué methods referenced in the projects. Even when a specific method of appliqué is suggested in the projects, you are always free to substitute your favorite method. Just be sure to adapt the pattern pieces and project instructions as necessary.

Making Templates

To begin, you will need to make templates of the appliqué patterns. Templates made from clear plastic are more durable and accurate than those made from cardboard. Since you can see through the plastic, it is easy to trace the templates accurately.

Place template plastic over each pattern piece and trace with a fine-line permanent marker. Do not add seam allowances. Cut out the templates on the drawn lines. You need only one template for each different motif or shape. Write the pattern name and grain-line arrow (if applicable) on the template.

Marking and Cutting Fabric

Place the template right side up on the right side of the appliqué fabric. Trace around the template, leaving at least ½" between tracings if several pieces are needed. Cut out each fabric piece, adding a scant ¼"-wide seam allowance around the traced line. This seam allowance will be turned under to create the finished edge of the appliqué. On very small pieces, you may wish to add only ⅛" for easier handling.

The appliqué pieces that you cut out are sewn to a background block, which is usually a rectangle or square. Cut the background blocks the size and shape required for each project. In some cases, especially in those involving more detailed appliqué, the cut measurement for the background block has been enlarged an inch in each direction, with instructions to trim it to the correct size after the appliqué has been sewn in place.

An appliqué placement diagram is provided for each quilt that involves an appliqué design. In some cases this diagram is the actual size and may be traced directly on the background block for guidance in positioning the appliqués. Place the background block right side up over the diagram so that the appliqué design is centered. Lightly trace the design with a pencil. If your background fabric is dark, use a light box, or try taping the diagram to a window or storm door on a sunny day.

When a full-size diagram is not provided, simply use the scaled-down illustration, along with the color photo of the quilt, as a model for positioning the appliqué pieces.

Traditional Appliqué Method

Before sewing appliqués to the background block, turn under the seam allowances along the traced lines. Next, baste around each piece. Look at the right side of the piece while you turn the seam allowance under, and baste right along the fold to catch the seam allowance.

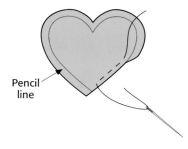

Pencil line

Do not turn under edges that will be covered by other appliqué pieces. They should lie flat under the covering appliqué piece.

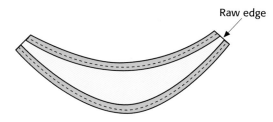

Raw edge

Pin or baste the appliqués to the background block. If you have trouble with threads tangling around pins as you sew, try placing the pins on the underside of your work.

Traditional Appliqué Stitch

The traditional appliqué stitch or blind stitch is appropriate for sewing all appliqué shapes, including sharp points and curves. The following steps describe the process.

1. Thread the needle with an 18" (approximate) single strand of thread in a color that closely matches the color of the appliqué. Knot the thread tail.

2. Hide the knot by slipping the needle into the seam allowance from the wrong side of the appliqué piece, bringing it out on the fold line.

3. Work from right to left if you are right-handed, or from left to right if you are left-handed.

4. Start the first stitch by moving the needle straight off the appliqué, inserting the needle into the background block. Let the needle travel under the background, parallel to the edge of the appliqué; bring it up about ⅛" away.

5. As you bring the needle up, pierce the basted edge of the appliqué piece, catching only one or two threads of the edge.

6. Move the needle straight off the appliqué into the background block. Let your needle travel under the background, bringing it up about ⅛" away, again catching the basted edge of the appliqué.

7. Give the thread a slight tug and continue stitching.

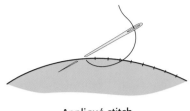

Appliqué stitch

Note: The stitches in these appliqué illustrations show placement. The stiches should not show in the completed work.

8. To end your stitching, pull the needle through to the wrong side. Behind the appliqué piece, take 2 small stitches, making knots by taking your needle through the loops. Check the right side to see if the thread shows through the background. If it does, take one more small stitch on the back side to direct the tail of the thread under the appliqué fabric.

Stitching Outside Points

As you stitch toward an outside point on the appliqué piece, start taking smaller stitches within ½" of the point. Trim the seam allowance or push the excess fabric under the point with the tip of your needle. Smaller stitches near the point will keep any frayed edges from escaping.

Place the last stitch on the first side of the point, very close to the point. Place the next stitch on the second side of the point. These stitches on each side, close to the point, accent the point.

Stitching Along a Curve

Push the fabric under with the tip of your needle, smoothing it out along the folded edge before sewing.

Stitching Inside Points

Make your stitches smaller as you sew within ½" of the point. Stitch past the point; then return to the point to add one extra stitch to emphasize it. Come up through the appliqué, catching a little more fabric in the inside point (four or five threads instead of one or two). Make a straight stitch outward, going under the point to pull it in a little and emphasize its shape.

If your inside point frays, sew a few stitches close together to tack the fabric down securely. If your thread matches your appliqué fabric, these stitches will blend in with the edge of the shape.

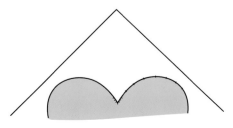

Alternate Appliqué Methods

Needle-Turn Appliqué

This method moves directly from cutting to the appliqué stitch. You do not turn under and baste the seam allowances. The following steps describe the process.

1. Using a plastic template, trace the appliqué design onto the right side of the appliqué fabric.
2. Cut out the fabric piece, adding a scant $\frac{1}{4}$"-wide seam allowance all around.
3. Position the appliqué piece on the background fabric or block; pin or baste the appliqué in place.
4. Starting on a straight edge, use the tip of the needle to gently turn under the seam allowance, about $\frac{1}{2}$" at a time. Hold the turned seam allowance firmly between the thumb and first finger of your left hand (reverse if left-handed) as you stitch the appliqué to the background block. Use a longer needle—a Sharp or Milliner's—to help you control the seam allowance and turn it under neatly.

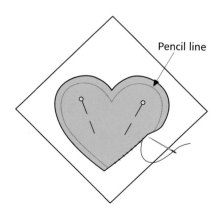

Pencil line

Freezer-Paper Appliqué

Freezer paper (coated on one side) is often used to help make perfectly shaped appliqués. The following is a step-by-step explanation of the process.

1. Trace around the template on the paper side, not the shiny side, of the freezer paper with a sharp pencil; or place the freezer paper, shiny side down, on top of the pattern and trace.

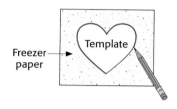

Template

Freezer paper

2. Cut out the traced design on the pencil line. Do not add seam allowances.
3. With the shiny side against the wrong side of a piece of appliqué fabric, iron the freezer-paper cutout in place with a hot, dry iron.

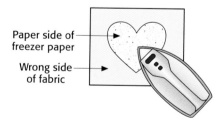

Paper side of freezer paper

Wrong side of fabric

4. Cut out the fabric shape, adding ¼"-wide seam allowances all around the outside edge of the freezer paper.

5. Turn and baste the seam allowance over the freezer-paper edges by hand, or use a fabric gluestick. Clip inside points and fold outside points.

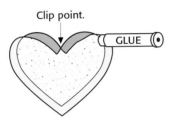

Clip point.

GLUE

6. Pin or baste the design to the background fabric or block. Appliqué the design.

7. Remove any basting stitches. Cut a small slit in the background fabric behind the appliqué and remove the freezer paper with tweezers. If you used a gluestick, soak the piece in warm water for a few minutes before removing the freezer paper.

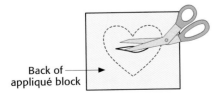

Back of appliqué block

Making Bias Stems for Appliqué

Bias stems are easy to make with the help of metal or nylon bias press bars. These handy notions are available at most quilt shops. The following steps describe the process of making bias stems.

1. Cut a piece of fabric as instructed in the specific quilt instructions. Cut the fabric into 1¼"-wide bias strips, using a rotary cutter and clear acrylic ruler.

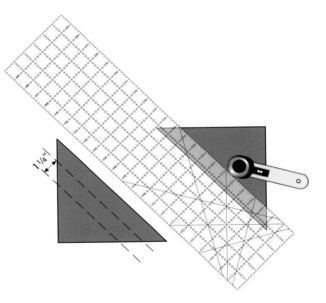

1¼"

2. Fold each strip in half lengthwise, wrong sides together. Stitch ½" from the folded edge. This will leave a ⅛" seam allowance.

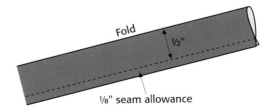

Fold

½"

⅛" seam allowance

3. Insert a $\frac{1}{2}$" bias bar, roll the seam to the underside, and press flat. Remove the bias bar. The finished strip will measure $\frac{1}{2}$" wide, the size required for the projects in this book.

Bias bar

Assembling the Quilt Top

Squaring Up Blocks

When your blocks are complete, take the time to square them up. Use a large square ruler to measure your blocks and make sure they are the desired size plus an exact $\frac{1}{4}$" on each edge for seam allowances. For example, if you are making $8\frac{1}{2}$" blocks, they should all measure 9" before you sew them together. Trim the larger blocks to match the size of the smallest one. Be sure to trim all four sides; otherwise your block will be lopsided.

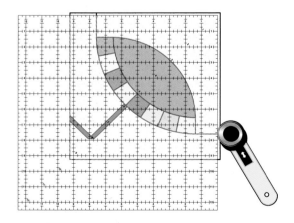

If your blocks are not the required finished size, adjust all the other components of the quilt accordingly.

Making Straight-Set Quilts

The following steps describe how to sew together a straight-set quilt.

1. Arrange the blocks as shown in the quilt assembly diagram included with the quiltmaking instructions.
2. Sew the blocks together in horizontal rows; press the seams in opposite directions from row to row.
3. Sew the rows together, making sure to match the seams between the blocks.

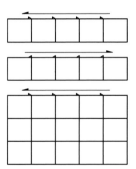

Straight-set quilts

Making Diagonally Set Quilts

The following steps describe how to sew together a diagonally set quilt.

1. Arrange the blocks, side setting triangles, and corner setting triangles as shown in the quilt assembly diagram provided with each quilt.
2. Sew the blocks and side setting triangles together in diagonal rows; press the seams in opposite directions from row to row.
3. Sew the rows together, making sure to match the seams between the blocks. Sew the corner setting triangles on last.

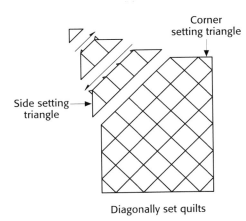

Diagonally set quilts

Adding Borders

For best results, do not cut border strips and sew them directly to the quilt without measuring first. The edges of a quilt often measure slightly longer than the distance through the quilt center, due to stretching during construction. Instead, measure the quilt top through the center in both directions to determine how long to cut the border strips. This step ensures that the finished quilt will be as straight and as "square" as possible, without wavy edges.

Many of the quilts in this book call for plain border strips. These strips are cut along the crosswise grain and seamed where extra length is needed.

Borders may have straight-cut corners or corner squares. Check the quilt pattern you are following.

The following sections describe how to add the two different kinds of borders.

Straight-Cut Borders

1. Measure the length of the quilt top through the center. From the crosswise grain, cut 2 border strips to that measurement, piecing as necessary. Mark the center of the quilt edges and the border strips. Pin the borders to opposite sides of the quilt top, matching the center marks and ends and easing as necessary. Sew the border strips in place. Press the seams toward the border.

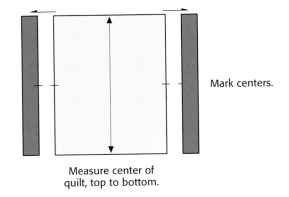

Mark centers.

Measure center of quilt, top to bottom.

2. Measure the width of the quilt top through the center, including the side borders just added. From the crosswise grain, cut 2 border strips to that measurement, piecing as necessary. Mark the

center of the quilt edges and the border strips. Pin the borders to the top and bottom edges of the quilt top, matching the center marks and ends and easing as necessary. Sew the border strips in place. Press the seams toward the border.

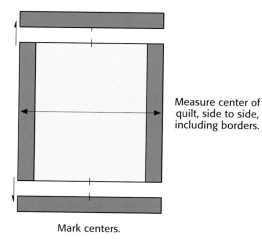

Measure center of quilt, side to side, including borders.

Mark centers.

Borders with Corner Squares

1. Measure the width and length of the quilt top through the center. From the crosswise grain, cut border strips to those measurements, piecing as necessary. Mark the center of the quilt edges and the border strips. Pin the side borders to opposite sides of the quilt top, matching centers and ends and easing as necessary. Sew the side border strips; press the seams toward the border.

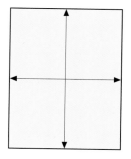

2. Cut corner squares of the required size, which is the cut width of the border strips. Sew 1 corner square to each end of the remaining 2 border strips; press the seams toward the border strips. Pin the border strips to the top and bottom edges of the quilt top. Match centers, seams between the border strips and corner squares, and ends. Ease as necessary and stitch. Press the seams toward the border.

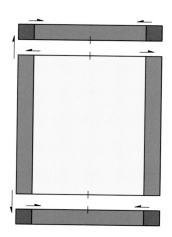

◆ Preparing to Quilt

Marking the Quilting Lines

Whether you mark quilting designs on the quilt top or not depends upon the type of quilting you will be doing. Marking is not necessary if you plan to quilt in the ditch (along the seam lines) or outline quilt a uniform distance from seam lines. For more complex quilting designs, however, mark the quilt top before the quilt is layered with batting and backing.

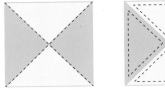

Quilting in the ditch   Outline quilting

Choose a marking tool that will be visible on your fabric and test it on fabric scraps to be sure the marks can be removed easily. See "Marking Tools" on page 7 for options. Masking tape can be used to mark straight quilting lines. Tape only small sections at a time and remove the tape when you stop at the end of the day; otherwise, the sticky residue may be difficult to remove from the fabric.

Layering the Quilt

Once you complete the quilt top and mark it for quilting, assemble the quilt "sandwich," which consists of the backing, batting, and the quilt top. The quilt backing and batting should be at least 4" larger than the quilt top

all the way around. For large quilts, it is usually necessary to sew two or three lengths of fabric together to make a backing that is large enough. Trim away the selvages before piecing the lengths together. Press the seams open to make quilting easier.

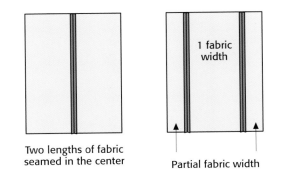

Two lengths of fabric seamed in the center   1 fabric width   Partial fabric width

Batting comes packaged in standard bed sizes, or it can be purchased by the yard. Several weights or thicknesses are available. Thick battings are fine for tied quilts and comforters; a thinner batting is better, however, if you intend to quilt by hand or machine.

The following steps describe how to layer the quilt.

Basting

1. Spread the backing, wrong side up, on a flat, clean surface. Anchor it with pins or masking tape. Be careful not to stretch the backing out of shape.

2. Spread the batting over the backing, smoothing out any wrinkles.

3. Center the pressed quilt top on top of the batting. Smooth out any wrinkles and make sure the quilt-top edges are parallel to the edges of the backing.

4. Starting in the center, baste with needle and thread and work diagonally to each corner. Continue basting in a grid of horizontal and vertical lines 6" to 8" apart. Finish by basting around the edges.

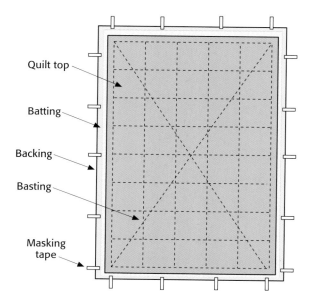

Note: For machine quilting, you may baste the layers with #2 rust-proof safety pins. Place pins about 6" to 8" apart, away from the areas you intend to quilt.

◢ Quilting Techniques

Hand Quilting

To quilt by hand, you will need short, sturdy needles (called Betweens), quilting thread, and a thimble to fit the middle finger of your sewing hand. Most quilters also use a frame or hoop to support their work. Use the smallest needle you can comfortably handle; the finer the needle, the smaller your stitches will be. The following steps explain how to hand quilt. For more information on hand

quilting, refer to *Loving Stitches: A Guide to Fine Hand Quilting* by Jeana Kimball (That Patchwork Place, 1992).

1. Thread your needle with a single strand of quilting thread about 18" long. Make a small knot and insert the needle in the top layer about 1" from the place where you want to start stitching. Pull the needle out at the point where quilting will begin and gently pull the thread until the knot pops through the fabric and into the batting.

2. Take small, evenly spaced stitches through all 3 quilt layers. Rock the needle up and down through all layers, until you have 3 or 4 stitches on the needle. Place your other hand underneath the quilt so you can feel the needle point with the tip of your finger when a stitch is taken.

3. To end a line of quilting, make a small knot close to the last stitch; then backstitch, running the thread a needle's length through the batting. Gently pull the thread until the knot pops into the batting; clip the thread at the quilt's surface.

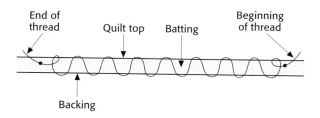

Machine Quilting

Machine quilting is suitable for all types of quilts, from crib to full-size bed quilts. With machine quilting, you can quickly complete quilts that might otherwise languish on the shelves.

Marking the quilting design is only necessary if you need to follow a grid or a complex pattern. It is not necessary if you plan to quilt in the ditch, outline quilt a uniform distance from seam lines, or free-motion quilt in a random pattern.

For straight-line quilting, it is extremely helpful to have a walking foot to help feed the quilt layers through the machine without shifting or puckering. Some machines have a built-in walking foot; other machines require a separate attachment.

Walking foot

For free-motion quilting, you need a darning foot and the ability to drop the feed dogs on your machine. With free-motion quilting, you guide the fabric in the direction of the design rather than turn the fabric under the needle. Use free-motion quilting to outline quilt a fabric motif or to create stippling or other curved designs.

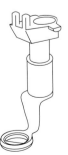

Darning foot

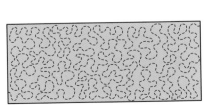

Free-motion quilting

Button Tufting

Using buttons is a quick and easy way to secure the layers of a quilt. You can use buttons in the same colors as the quilt, or you can use contrasting colors for fun. Shaped buttons, such as stars, flowers, and hearts, can also add another dimension to the quilt.

To tack with buttons, lower the feed dogs on your sewing machine and set the stitch length at 0. Adjust the stitch width to match the holes in each button. Stitch the buttons, tacking through all three layers.

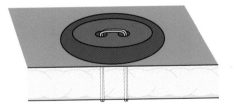

CAUTION

Do not use buttons on quilts for young children, since buttons can be pulled off.

◆ Finishing

Binding

The instructions for the quilts in this book call for binding made from strips of fabric cut on the straight of grain or bias.

For straight-grain, French double-fold binding, cut strips 2½" wide across the width of the fabric. You will need enough strips to go around the perimeter of the quilt plus 10" for seams and to turn the corners.

For bias-grain binding, follow these steps:

1. Fold the square of fabric designated for the binding on the diagonal.

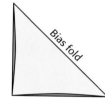

   OR

   Fold a ½-yard piece as shown in the diagrams below, paying careful attention to the location of the lettered corners.

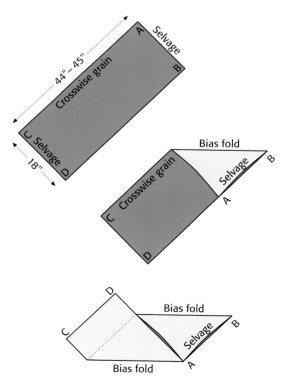

2. Cut strips 2¼" wide, cutting perpendicular to the folds as shown.

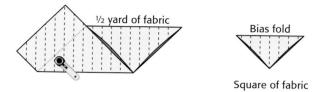

To join the strips and attach the binding, follow these steps:

1. With right sides together, join strips at right angles and stitch across the corner as shown. Trim excess fabric and press the seams open to make one long piece of binding.

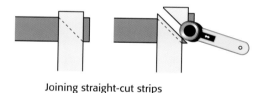

Joining straight-cut strips

Joining bias strips

2. If necessary, trim one end of the strip at a 45° angle. Turn under ¼" and press. Fold the strip in half lengthwise, wrong sides together, and press.

3. Trim the batting and backing even with the quilt top.

4. Starting on one side of the quilt (not a corner!) and using a $\frac{1}{4}$"-wide seam allowance, stitch the binding to the quilt, keeping the raw edges even with the quilt top edge. End the stitching $\frac{1}{4}$" from the corner of the quilt and backstitch. Clip the thread.

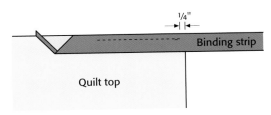

5. Turn the quilt so you will be stitching down the next side. Fold the binding up, away from the quilt, with raw edges aligned.

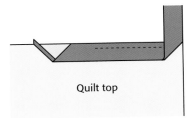

6. Fold the binding back down onto itself, even with the edge of the quilt top. Begin stitching $\frac{1}{4}$" from the corner, backstitching to secure the stitches.

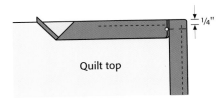

7. Repeat the process on the remaining edges and corners of the quilt. When you reach the beginning of the binding, stop stitching. Overlap the starting edge of the binding by about 1" and cut away any excess binding, trimming the end at a 45° angle. Tuck the end of the binding into the fold and finish the seam.

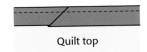

8. Fold the binding over the raw edges of the quilt to the back of the quilt, with the folded edge covering the row of machine stitching. Blindstitch the binding in place. A miter will form at each corner. Blindstitch the mitered corners in place.

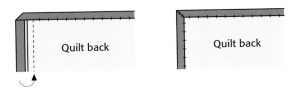

Signing Your Quilt

Be sure to sign and date your quilt. Future generations will be interested to know more than just who made it and when. Labels can be as elaborate or as simple as you desire. The information can be handwritten, typed, or embroidered. Be sure to include the name of the quilt, your name, your city and state, the date, the name of the recipient if it is a gift, and any other interesting or important information about the quilt.

Heart blocks are one of my favorites, and I like to think of interesting ways to make them. As a lover of folk art, I prefer scrap quilts made with many fabrics. I would rather use fifteen different red fabrics in a quilt than just one red fabric fifteen times. In this quilt, I was able to combine my love of hearts with many different '30s red and blue prints. Because I don't often use yellow, I challenged myself to use it this time. It adds light and energy to the lively blues and reds.

Sandy Bonsib

Finished quilt size: 39½" × 47¾"
Finished block size: 5¾"

Materials

42"-wide fabric

½ yd. *total* of assorted red prints for pieced blocks

1½ yds. light yellow solid for pieced blocks and border

1⅓ yds. *total* of assorted '30s blue prints for plain blocks, setting triangles, and corner setting triangles

⅔ yd. red plaid for binding

1½ yds. fabric for backing

44" × 52" piece of batting

Red perle cotton, size 8 (optional)

Size 24 chenille needle (optional)

Cutting

All measurements include ¼"-wide seam allowances.

From the assorted red prints, cut:
    A *total* of 40 rectangles, each 2½" × 4½", for pieced blocks

From the light yellow solid, cut:
    2 strips, each 3½" × 41¼", for side borders
    2 strips, each 3½" × 39¼", for top and bottom borders
    40 squares, each 2½" × 2½", for pieced blocks
    80 squares, each 1½" × 1½", for pieced blocks
    40 squares, each 4" × 4", for pieced blocks

From the assorted '30s blue prints, cut:
    A *total* of 12 squares, each 6¼" × 6¼", for plain blocks
    A *total* of 4 squares, each 10" × 10", for side setting triangles
    A *total* of 2 squares, each 6" × 6", for corner setting triangles

From the red plaid, cut:
    1 square, 24" × 24", for bias binding

My Heart Belongs to the '30s
By Sandy Bonsib, 1999, Issaquah, Washington
Quilted by Becky Kraus

◆ Making the Pieced Blocks

You'll need 20 pieced heart blocks for this quilt. Refer to "Machine Piecing" on page 9 for general piecing techniques.

1. Draw a diagonal line on the wrong side of the 1½" and the 2½" yellow squares.

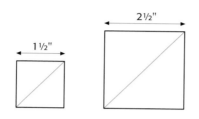

2. With right sides together, align a 1½" yellow square with the upper *left* corner of each 2½" × 4½" red rectangle as shown. Stitch directly on the drawn line and trim away the excess, leaving a ¼" seam allowance. Press the triangle toward the corner.

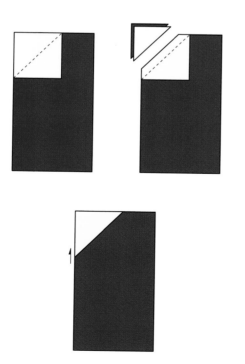

3. Repeat step 2 to add a 1½" yellow square to the upper *right* corner of each red rectangle as shown.

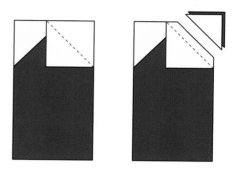

4. With right sides together, align a 2½" yellow square with the bottom edge of a pieced rectangle. Be sure the square is positioned so that the diagonal line runs from the upper left corner to the lower right corner. Stitch directly on the drawn line and trim away the excess, leaving a ¼" seam allowance. Press the triangle toward the corner. Make 20 of these units.

Make 20.

5. Repeat step 4 to sew a 2½" yellow square to the bottom of the remaining 20 pieced rectangle units. This time, be sure the square is positioned so that the diagonal line runs from the upper right corner to the lower left corner.

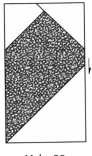

Make 20.

6. With right sides together, pin and sew rectangle units from steps 4 and 5 in pairs to form Heart blocks as shown. Press. Make 20.

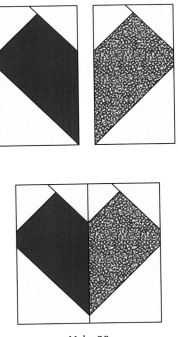

Make 20.

7. Cut each 4" yellow square in half once diagonally for a total of 80 triangles (see step 4 on page 8). Finger press each triangle to find its center. Match the center of the triangle with the center of the top and bottom of each Heart block, pin carefully, and sew. Press the seams toward the triangles.

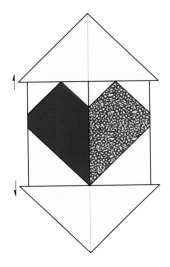

8. Pin and sew yellow triangles to both sides of each Heart block, once again matching centers and pressing the seams toward the triangles. Trim all Heart blocks to 6¼" × 6¼".

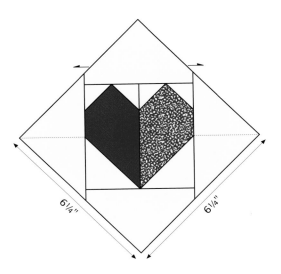

9. If desired, stitch a running stitch approximately ¼" from the outside edge of a few hearts, using the chenille needle and a strand of red perle cotton.

🔷 Assembling the Quilt

1. Referring to step 5 on page 8, cut each 10" blue print square twice diagonally to make 16 side setting triangles.

2. Referring to step 4 on page 8, cut each 6" blue print square in half diagonally to make 4 corner setting triangles.

3. Refer to the quilt assembly diagram below and the color photo on page 25 to arrange the pieced Heart blocks, 6¼" blue print plain blocks, side setting triangles, and corner setting triangles in a pleasing and balanced color arrangement.

Note: You'll have 2 side setting triangles left over.

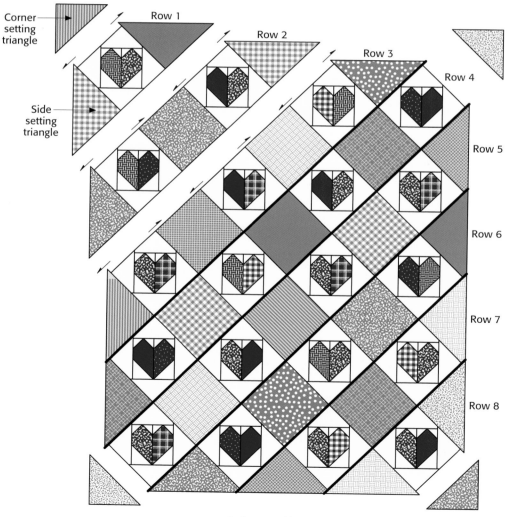

Quilt Assembly Diagram

4. Pin, then sew the Heart blocks, plain blocks, and side setting triangles to make 8 diagonal rows. Press all seams away from the pieced blocks (see "Making Diagonally Set Quilts" on page 7).

5. Carefully pin the rows together, matching the seams; then sew the rows together. Press. Add the 4 corner setting triangles to complete the quilt center.

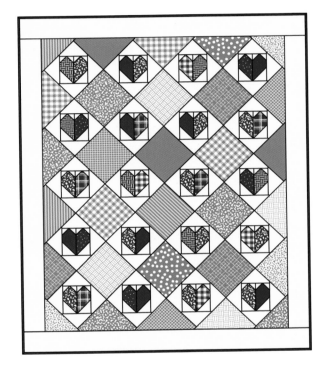

Sandy's Tip

I oversize my setting and corner setting triangles a bit for accuracy, so you may need to use your rotary cutter to straighten the edges of the quilt top before adding the borders.

6. Referring to "Adding Borders" on pages 17–18, pin and sew the 3½" × 41¼" border strips to the sides of the quilt. Press the seams toward the border strips. Repeat to pin and sew the 3½" × 39¼" border strips to the top and bottom edges of the quilt. Press the seams toward the border strips.

◆ Finishing

1. Referring to "Layering the Quilt" on page 19, center and layer the quilt top and the batting over the backing; baste.

2. Quilt as desired (see "Quilting Techniques" on pages 20–21). Becky outlined a few of the hearts with red thread and quilted a variety of motifs—including subtle hearts—in blue thread on the plain blocks and setting triangles. She finished the quilt by quilting a high-contrast red vine in the yellow border.

3. Trim the batting and backing even with the edges of the quilt top. Refer to the instructions for bias-grain binding on page 22 to cut 2¼"-wide bias strips from the 24" red plaid square, for a total of approximately 185" of bias binding. Sew the binding strips to the quilt.

4. Make and attach a label to the quilt.

PIECES OF THE PAST

I have always had an affinity for quilts from the '30s. When I was growing up, I slept under a quilt made in the '30s by my great grandmother. It was a Dresden Plate appliquéd on a blue background. My favorite part of the quilt was a small section where a seam had split, exposing the batting and stitches inside the quilt. I think that sleeping under that quilt helped make me a quilter!

Mimi Dietrich

Finished quilt size: $25\frac{1}{2}$" × $32\frac{1}{2}$"
Finished block size: $3\frac{1}{2}$"

Materials

42"-wide fabric

1 yd. *total* of assorted '30s solids and prints in blue, pink, green, yellow, lavender, and teal

$\frac{1}{4}$ yd. pink solid for inner borders and appliqué hearts

$\frac{1}{2}$ yd. blue '30s print for outer borders

$\frac{1}{4}$ yd. blue solid for binding

1 yd. fabric for backing

29" × 36" piece of batting

18 antique buttons or replicas of antique buttons

Cutting

All measurements include $\frac{1}{4}$"-wide seam allowances.

From the assorted '30s prints, cut:

A *total* of 17 squares, each 4" × 4", for appliqué background and plain blocks

A *total* of 9 squares, each $4\frac{3}{4}$" × $4\frac{3}{4}$", for pieced blocks*

From the assorted '30s solids, cut:

A *total* of 9 squares, each $4\frac{3}{4}$" × $4\frac{3}{4}$", for pieced blocks**

From the pink solid, cut:

2 strips, each $1\frac{1}{4}$" × 25", for side inner borders

2 strips, each $1\frac{1}{4}$" × $19\frac{1}{2}$", for top and bottom inner borders

From the blue '30s print, cut:

2 strips, each $3\frac{1}{2}$" × $26\frac{1}{2}$", for side outer borders

2 strips, each $3\frac{1}{2}$" × $25\frac{1}{2}$", for top and bottom outer borders

From the blue solid, cut:

3 strips, each $2\frac{1}{2}$" × 42", for binding

*Two of the squares should be blue prints to make the center star in the quilt.
**Two of the squares should be blue solids to make the center star in the quilt.

Pieces of the Past
By Mimi Dietrich, 1999, Baltimore, Maryland

◆ Making the Appliqué Blocks

You'll need 2 appliqué Heart blocks for this quilt. Refer to "Basic Appliqué" on pages 11–16 for general appliqué techniques. Choose the appliqué method you prefer and follow the instructions appropriate to that method.

1. Refer to "Marking and Cutting Fabric" on page 11 and use the appliqué placement diagram below to prepare and mark two 4" print background squares for appliqué.

2. Use the heart pattern below to make a template. Trace the template and cut 2 hearts from the pink solid fabric, adding a scant ¼"-wide seam allowance around the traced line as you cut.

3. Using your preferred method, position and appliqué a heart in the center of each marked background block. Make 2 blocks.

Heart
Cut 2

Pieces of the Past
Pattern and
Appliqué Placement Diagram

◗ Making the Pieced Blocks

You'll need a total of 18 pieced blocks for this quilt. Refer to "Machine Piecing" starting on page 9 for general piecing techniques. Be sure that 4 of the blocks are sewn with blue prints and solids to create the center star.

1. Referring to step 5 on page 18, cut each 4¾" print square twice diagonally for a total of 36 triangles. Repeat with the 4¾" solid squares.
2. Match 1 print triangle with 1 solid triangle that is the same color to make a pair. With right sides together, pin and sew along one short side. Press the seam toward the solid triangle. Repeat to make a second identical pair.

3. Place the 2 triangle units from step 2 right sides together. Be sure that the triangles are opposite—print to solid, solid to print. Pin carefully to match the center seam. Sew the 2 units together along the diagonal edge to make a block, and press. Make a total of 18 pieced blocks.

Make 18.

◗ Assembling the Quilt

1. Refer to the quilt assembly diagram below, the color photo on page 31, and "Making Straight-Set Quilts" on page 16 to arrange alternating pieced and plain blocks in 7 horizontal rows of 5 blocks each. Odd number rows begin with pieced blocks, while even numbered rows begin with plain blocks. Note that an appliqué block replaces a plain block in rows 3 and 5, and that 4 pieced blue blocks form the center star in rows 3, 4, and 5.

Quilt Assembly Diagram

2. With right sides together, pin and sew the blocks together into rows. Press the seams toward the plain or appliquéd blocks.

3. Carefully pin the rows together, matching the seams; then join the rows and press.

4. Referring to "Adding Borders" on pages 17–18, pin and sew the 1¼" × 25" pink inner border strips to the sides of the quilt. Press the seams toward the border strips. Repeat to pin and sew the 1¼" × 19½" pink inner border strips to the top and bottom edges of the quilt. Press the seams toward the border strips.

5. Pin and sew the 3½" × 26½" blue outer border strips to the sides of the quilt. Press the seams toward the border strips. Repeat to sew the 3½" × 25½" outer border strips to the top and bottom edges of the quilt top. Press the seams toward the border strips.

Detail of quilt center

✦ Finishing

1. Referring to "Layering the Quilt" on page 19, center and layer the quilt top and the batting over the backing; baste.

2. Quilt as desired (see "Quilting Techniques" on pages 20–21). Mimi's quilt was quilted in the ditch around the pieced blocks and outline quilted around the appliquéd hearts. A simple quilted cable design completes the border.

3. Trim the batting and backing even with the edges of the quilt top. Referring to "Binding" on pages 22–23, use the 2½" × 42" blue solid strips to make the binding; then sew the binding to the quilt.

4. Stitch a button in the center of each pieced block as shown in the photo on page 34.

5. Make and attach a label to your finished quilt. An appliqué heart makes a fine label for this quilt. Enlarge the pattern on page 32 and trace the heart shape. Embellish with calligraphy, embroidery, or other decorative stitching.

My goal in designing this quilt was to make it flexible and easy. With a scrap fabric approach and just nine paper-pieced blocks, I think I met my goal!

This colorful nosegay is reminiscent of the '30s, when frugal quilters often used scraps and other leftover bits and pieces. I used three fat quarters each of yellows, greens, blues, pinks, and purples to make this quilt, but random scraps would work just as easily. Make your version a smaller or larger quilt by making fewer or more blocks and border squares.

Carol Doak

Finished quilt size: 40½" × 40½"
Finished block size: 9"

◈ Material

42"-wide fabric

1⅛ yds. white tone-on-tone or solid for
   blocks and inner border
¼ yd. *each* of 3 different medium green,
   pink, blue, yellow, and purple '30s
   prints for blocks and pieced border*
½ yd. yellow fabric for binding
1¼ yds. fabric for backing
42" × 42" piece of batting
Size 90/14 sewing machine needle

*May be either traditional (9" × 42") or fat (18" × 22")
   quarters.

◈ Cutting for the Borders and Binding

All measurements include ¼"-wide seam allowances.

From the white fabric, cut:
   2 strips, each 2" × 27½", for side inner
      borders
   2 strips, each 2" × 30½", for top and
      bottom inner borders
From the assorted green '30s prints, cut:
   A *total* of 5 squares, each 5½" × 5½",
      for pieced border
From the assorted pink '30s prints, cut:
   A *total* of 8 squares, each 5½" × 5½",
      for pieced border
From the assorted blue '30s prints, cut:
   A *total* of 5 squares, each 5½" × 5½",
      for pieced border
From the assorted yellow '30s prints, cut:
   A *total* of 5 squares, each 5½" × 5½",
      for pieced border
From the assorted purple '30s prints, cut:
   A *total* of 5 squares, each 5½" × 5½",
      for pieced border
From the yellow binding fabric, cut:
   5 strips, each 2½" × 42"

Nosegays
By Carol Doak, 1999, Windham, New Hampshire

◢ Cutting for the Nosegay Blocks

Cut the following pieces for the Nosegay blocks. Label them with the location numbers. For each piece identified with ▱ , cut the squares in half diagonally (see step 4 on page 8). For each piece identified with an ⊠, cut the squares twice diagonally (see step 5 on page 8).

CUTTING CHART FOR NOSEGAY BLOCK (TOP)

Piece Number	Fabric	Dimensions	Number of Pieces
1	White	2½" × 2½"	9 (total)
4, 5	White	1½" × 4½"	18 (total)
8, 9, 12, 13	White	3" × 3" ⊠	9 squares (36 triangles total)
16, 17	White	2¾" × 2¾" ▱	9 squares (18 triangles total)
2	Assorted pink '30s prints	1½" × 2½"	9 (total)
3	Assorted pink '30s prints	2¼" × 4"	9 (total)
18	Assorted pink '30s prints	5¾" × 5¾" ▱ *	5 squares (10 triangles total)
6, 7	Assorted blue '30s prints	1¼" × 4"	18 (total)
19	Assorted blue '30s prints	5¾" × 5¾" ▱ *	5 squares (10 triangles total)
10, 11	Assorted yellow '30s prints	1¼" × 4"	18 (total)
14, 15	Assorted purple '30s prints	2" × 4½"	18 (total)

* You will have 1 extra triangle.
⊠ = cut squares twice diagonally
▱ = cut squares once diagonally

CUTTING CHART FOR NOSEGAY BLOCK (BOTTOM)

Piece Number	Fabric	Dimensions	Number of Pieces
2, 3	White	3" × 7¼"	18 (total)
1	Assorted green '30s prints	5¼" × 5¼"	9 (total)
5	Assorted yellow '30s prints	5¾" × 5¾" ▱ *	5 squares (10 triangles total)
4	Assorted purple '30s prints	5¾" × 5¾" ▱ *	5 squares (10 triangles total)

* You will have 1 extra triangle.
▱ = cut squares once diagonally

◆ Foundation Piecing the Nosegay Blocks

The Nosegay block is pieced in 2 sections with paper foundations. When completed, the 2 sections are joined to make a block. You'll need a total of 9 Nosegay blocks for this quilt. Refer to the color photo below for guidance in placing the colors within the blocks. As you can see, Carol randomly chose the prints for each block.

1. Make 9 copies of the patterns on pages 44–45 for the top and bottom of the Nosegay block. You may use a copy machine; however, make all the copies *from the original patterns* on the same photocopy machine. Trim the patterns ½" beyond the outside line.

Detail of Nosegay block

2. Prepare your sewing machine for paper foundation piecing by reducing the stitch length to approximately 18 to 20 stitches per inch. Install a size 90/14 needle.

3. Pin piece 1 right side up on the blank side of the paper pattern for the bottom of the Nosegay block, covering the area marked 1 plus at least ¼" on all sides.

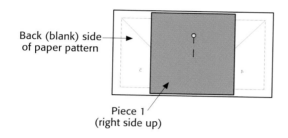

Back (blank) side of paper pattern

Piece 1
(right side up)

4. Flip the pattern to the printed side. Place a postcard on the seam line between the areas marked 1 and 2. Fold the paper over the edge of the card to expose the excess fabric of piece 1. Place the ¼" line on your rotary ruler directly on the fold. Trim the excess fabric of piece 1, leaving a ¼" seam allowance.

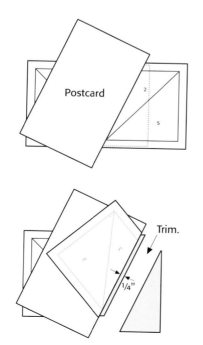

Postcard

Trim.

¼"

5. Place piece 2 right side up on the blank side of the paper pattern over the area marked 2. Make sure it is correctly positioned. Next, flip piece 2 so that the right sides of pieces 1 and 2 are together. Piece 2 should be flush with the just-trimmed edge of piece 1. Pin piece 2 to hold it in place.

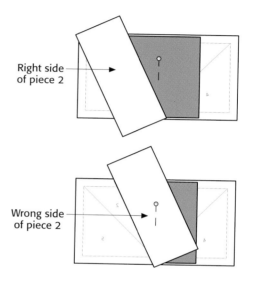

Right side of piece 2

Wrong side of piece 2

6. Turn the paper pattern over to the printed side and sew directly on the seam line between the areas marked 1 and 2. Extend the stitching approximately ¼" beyond each end of the line. Open piece 2 and press with a dry iron on the cotton setting.

Carol's Tip

Use a piece of scrap fabric on your pressing area to protect it from the possibility of ink transfer from the paper pattern.

7. With the printed side of the pattern facing up, place the postcard on the next seam line (the adjoining line for piece 3). Fold the paper back along the edge of the postcard and repeat the process described in steps 4 through 6. Continue in this manner until all the pieces have been added.

8. Trim the paper foundation ¼" beyond the outside line.

9. Refer to steps 3–8 for general directions on how to piece the top sections of the Nosegay blocks.

10. Pin the 2 halves of the Nosegay block right sides together with the edges flush, keeping the pins away from the seam line. Readjust the stitch length on your sewing machine to a long stitch, and machine baste the beginning, the center, and the end of the center seam. Remove the pins and check that you have a good match. If necessary, remove the basting and try again for a better match. When you are satisfied, restitch the entire seam line with the smaller stitch.

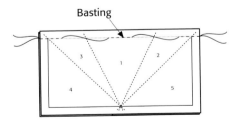

Basting

11. Press the middle seam allowance toward the bottom of the block. *Do not remove the paper foundations.*

Carol's Tip

Normally I would alternate the direction of the middle seam in the blocks; however, the multiple seam allowances in the top half of this block are happier being pressed toward the bottom!

Assembling the Quilt

1. Refer to the first diagram on page 42 and "Making Straight-Set Quilts" on page 16 to arrange the blocks in 3 horizontal rows of 3 blocks each.

2. With right sides together, pin the blocks together into rows. Refer to step 10 in "Foundation Piecing the Nosegay Blocks" (at left) to baste and check before sewing the blocks together with a small stitch. Sew the blocks into rows; then press the seams as indicated by the pressing arrows.

3. Carefully pin the rows together, matching the seams. Sew the rows together and press the seams as indicated by the pressing arrows.

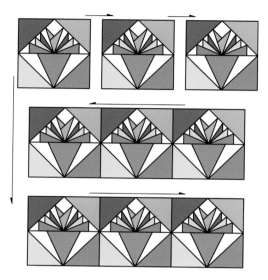

4. Referring to "Adding Borders" on pages 17–18, pin and sew the 2" × 27½" inner border strips to the sides of the quilt. Press the seams toward the border strips.

Repeat to pin and sew the 2" × 30½" inner border strips to the top and bottom edges of the quilt. Press the seams toward the border strips.

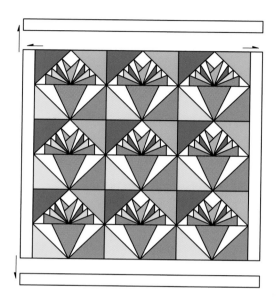

5. With right sides together, pin and sew the 5½" assorted squares together in rows. Press the seams as indicated in the quilt assembly diagram on page 43. Make 2 rows of 6 squares each, and 2 rows of 8 squares each. Refer to the color photo on page 37 for guidance.

6. Pin and sew the shorter (6 square) pieced border strips to the sides of the quilt. Press the seams toward the pieced borders. Repeat to sew the longer (8 square) border strips to the top and bottom edges of the quilt. Press the seams toward the pieced borders.

Quilt Assembly Diagram

Finishing

1. Carefully remove the paper from the foundation pieced blocks.
2. Referring to "Layering the Quilt" on page 19, center and layer the quilt top and the batting over the backing; baste.
3. Quilt as desired (see "Quilting Techniques" on pages 20–21).
4. Trim the batting and backing even with the edges of the quilt top. Referring to "Binding" on pages 22–23, use the 2½" × 42" yellow strips to make the binding; then sew the binding to the quilt.
5. Make and attach a label to your quilt.

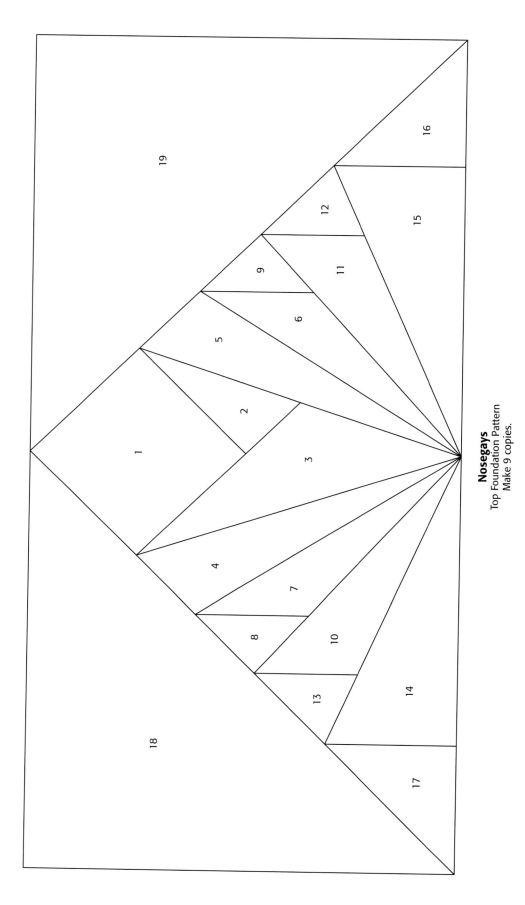

Nosegays
Top Foundation Pattern
Make 9 copies.

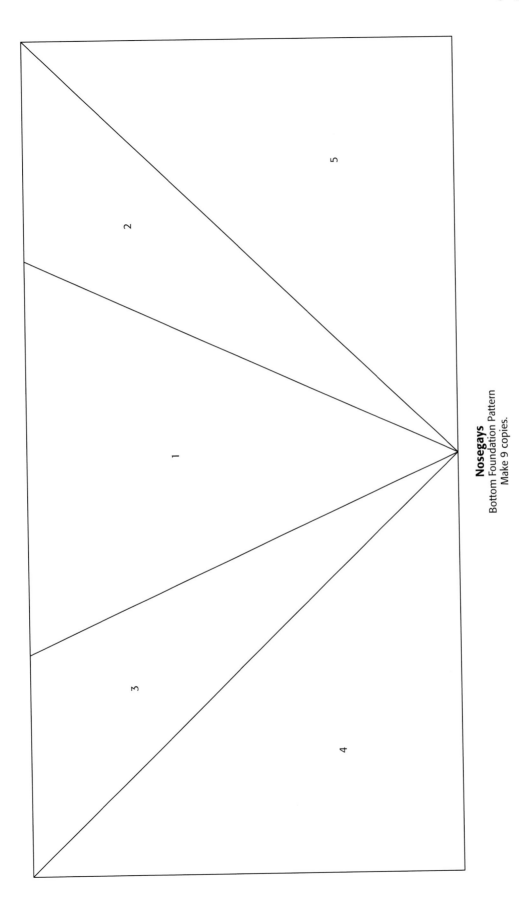

Nosegays
Bottom Foundation Pattern
Make 9 copies.

TRUE LOVER'S KNOT

The True Lover's Knot block was first published in one of my favorite books, *Romance of the Patchwork Quilt*, by Carrie Hall and Rose Kretsinger in 1935. True Lover's Knot has also been called Sassafras Leaf, Hand, and California Oak Leaf, but I prefer the more romantic name.

Nancy J. Martin

Finished quilt size: 57" × 57"
Finished block size: 14"

◆ Materials

42"-wide fabric

2 yds. light print for blocks, pieced sashing, and inner borders

1 fat quarter *each* of 6 assorted yellow '30s prints for blocks

1 fat quarter *each* of 6 assorted blue '30s prints for blocks

1 fat quarter *each* of 6 assorted green '30s prints for blocks

1 fat quarter *each* of 6 assorted pink '30s prints for blocks

1 fat quarter *each* of 4 assorted lavender '30s prints for blocks and pieced sashing

1 yd. light green '30s print for outer border

¾ yd. fabric for binding

3½ yds. fabric for backing

60" × 60" piece of batting

Assorted buttons for button tufting (optional)

◆ Cutting

All measurements include ¼"-wide seam allowances.

From the light print, cut:

11 strips, each 4½" × 20", for pieced sashing

6 strips, each 1½" × 42", for inner border

57 squares, each 2½" × 2½", for blocks and pieced sashing

24 strips, each 1½" × 20", for blocks

From *each* fat quarter of yellow, blue, green, and pink '30s prints, cut:

6 squares, each 2½" × 2½", for blocks

1 strip, 1½" × 20", for blocks

From *each* fat quarter of lavender '30s prints, cut:

6 strips, each 1½" × 20", for blocks and pieced sashing (You'll have a *total* of 2 strips left over.)

From the light green '30s print, cut:

6 strips, each 4¾" × 42", for outer border

From the binding fabric, cut:

1 square, 24" × 24", for bias binding

True Lover's Knot
By Nancy J. Martin, 1999, Woodinville, Washington

◼ Piecing the Blocks

You'll need 9 True Lover's Knot blocks for this quilt. Each block consists of yellow, blue, green, and pink Knot units, tied together with a lavender print "link." Additional lavender links form the pieced sashing strips that connect the blocks. Refer to "Machine Piecing" on pages 9–11 for general piecing techniques.

1. Pair each $1\frac{1}{2}$" × 20" light print strip with a $1\frac{1}{2}$" × 20" yellow, blue, green, or pink strip. With right sides together, sew along one long raw edge to make a total of 24 strip sets. Press all seams toward the colored strip. Each strip set should measure $2\frac{1}{2}$" × 20" when sewn and pressed.

2. Crosscut each strip set into six $2\frac{1}{2}$" segments. You'll have 144 segments.

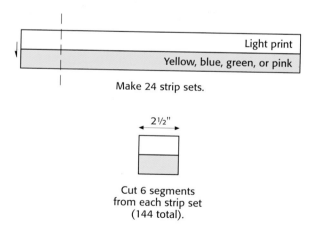

Light print

Yellow, blue, green, or pink

Make 24 strip sets.

2½"

Cut 6 segments
from each strip set
(144 total).

3. Arrange 4 same-color $2\frac{1}{2}$" squares, 4 crosscut segments, and a $2\frac{1}{2}$" light print square in 3 rows as shown.

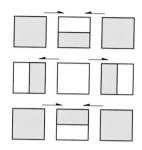

4. With right sides together, pin and sew the squares and crosscut segments into rows. Press the seams away from the squares. Carefully pin the rows together, matching the seams. Sew the rows together to make 1 Knot unit. Press. Make 9 Knot units of each color.

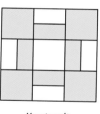

Knot unit
Make 9 in each color.

5. With right sides together and raw edges aligned, stitch a $1\frac{1}{2}$" × 20" lavender strip to each long side of a $4\frac{1}{2}$" × 20" light print strip to make a strip set. Press the seams toward the lavender strips. Make 11 strip sets. Each strip set should measure $6\frac{1}{2}$" × 20" when sewn and pressed.

6. Crosscut the strip sets into 2½"-wide segments. Cut a total of 78 link segments.

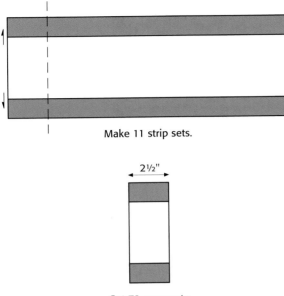

Make 11 strip sets.

2½"

Cut 78 segments.

7. Referring to the diagram below and the color photo at right, arrange a 2½" light print square, 1 Knot unit of each color (yellow, blue, green, and pink), and 4 lavender link segments in 3 rows as shown.

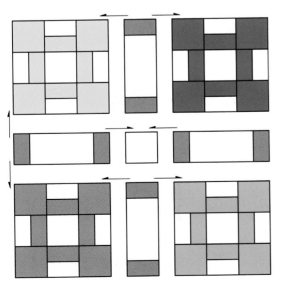

Make 9 blocks.

8. With right sides together, pin and sew the squares, Knot units, and links into rows. Press the seams away from the lavender links. Carefully pin the rows together, matching the seams; then sew the rows together. Press the seams away from the lavender links. Make 9 blocks.

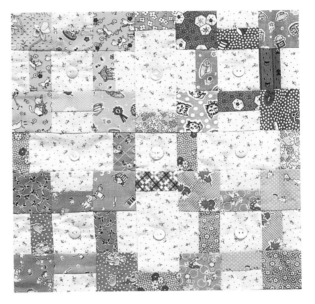

Detail of True Lover's Knot block

Making the Pieced Sashing

Place a 2½" light print square between 2 remaining lavender link segments as shown. Pin and sew to make a sashing unit. Press the seams toward the 2½" square. Make 12 sashing units.

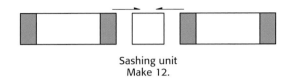

Sashing unit
Make 12.

Assembling the Quilt

1. Alternate 3 True Lover's Knot blocks with 2 sashing units to form a row as shown. Pin and sew the blocks and sashing units. Press the seams away from the sashing units. Make 3 rows.

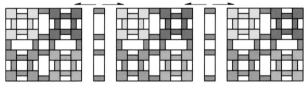

Make 3 rows.

2. Alternate 3 sashing units and two 2½" light print squares to form a row as shown. Pin and sew the units and squares. Press the seams toward the 2½" squares. Make 2 rows.

Make 2 rows.

3. Refer to the quilt assembly diagram at top right and "Making Straight-Set Quilts" on page 16 to arrange alternating block and sashing rows from step 1 and sashing

rows from step 2. Carefully pin the rows together, matching the seams; then sew the rows together and press.

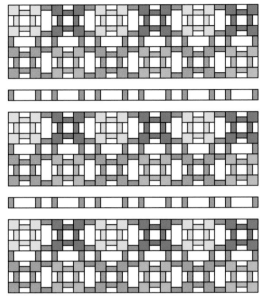

Quilt Assembly Diagram

4. Divide two 1½" × 42" inner border strips in half. Sew one half to each of the remaining 1½" × 42" inner border strips. Trim to make two 1½" × 46½" strips and two 1½" × 48½" strips.

5. Referring to "Adding Borders" on pages 17–18, pin and sew the 1½" × 46½" inner border strips to the sides of the quilt. Press the seams toward the border strips. Repeat to sew the 1½" × 48½" inner border strips to the top and bottom edges of the quilt. Press.

6. Repeat steps 4 and 5 with the 4¾" outer border strips to make two 4¾" × 48½" strips and two 4¾" × 57" strips. Pin and sew the shorter strips to the sides of the quilt, and the longer strips to the top and bottom edges of the quilt. Press the seams toward the outer borders.

🔹 Finishing

1. Choose a quilting design or plan the placement of buttons for button tufting (see "Button Tufting" on page 20). Depending on your selection, follow the directions in "Marking the Quilting Lines" on page 19 to prepare the quilt top for quilting.

2. Divide the backing fabric crosswise into 2 equal panels of approximately 63" each. Remove the selvages and join the pieces to make a single large backing panel.

3. Referring to "Layering the Quilt" on page 19, center and layer the quilt top and the batting over the backing; baste.

4. Quilt as desired (see "Quilting Techniques" on pages 20–21) or button tuft. To tack with buttons, lower the feed dogs, adjust the stitch width, and bar tack each button through all layers.

5. Trim the batting and backing even with the edges of the quilt top. Refer to the instructions for bias-grain binding on page 22 to cut 2¼"-wide bias strips from the 24" square of binding fabric, for a total of approximately 238" of bias binding. Sew the binding strips to the quilt.

6. Make and attach a label to the quilt.

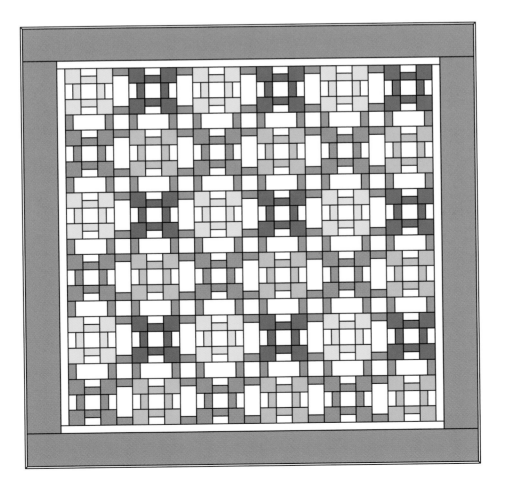

have been fascinated with Ruby McKim patterns for a long time. The black and white illustrations leave the world open for personal interpretation. When an opportunity to do a '30s quilt came up, it was the perfect chance to take this quilt off my someday list and make it with these '30s reproduction fabrics.

Cleo Nollette

Finished quilt size: 50½" × 50½"
Finished block size: 16"

Materials

42"-wide fabric

1⅛ yds. muslin or white fabric for appliqué background

1½ yds. green solid for stem and leaf appliqués, and binding

1 fat quarter *each* of four '30s prints for flower appliqués, Yo-yos, and pieced sashing

1 fat eighth *each* of three '30s prints for pieced sashing

1 yd. coordinating '30s print for outer border

3 yds. fabric for backing

54" × 54" piece of batting

Cleo's Tip

To give your quilt a more scrappy look, use as many different colors and '30s prints as you'd like for the flowers and pieced sashing strips.

Cutting

All measurements include ¼"-wide seam allowances.

From the muslin or white fabric, cut:

   4 oversized blocks, each 17½" × 17½", for appliqué background blocks

From the green solid, cut:

   1 square, 24" × 24", for bias stems

   1 square, 24" × 24", for bias binding

From the 4 fat quarters and 3 fat eighths, cut:

   A *total* of 105 squares, each 2½" × 2½", for pieced sashing

From the coordinating '30s print, cut:

   3 strips, each 6½" × 42", for top and bottom outer borders

   2 strips, each 6½" × 38½", for the side outer borders

Hollyhock Wreath
By Cleo Nollette, 1999, Seattle, Washington

◾ Appliquéing the Blocks

You'll need 4 appliqué Wreath blocks for this quilt. Refer to "Basic Appliqué" starting on page 11 for general appliqué techniques.

1. Carefully press each 17½" background square in half and then in quarters to establish guidelines for centering the appliqué design. Refer to "Marking and Cutting Fabric" on page 11 and use the appliqué placement diagram below to prepare and mark the 4 background squares for appliqué.

Appliqué Placement Diagram

2. Refer to "Making Bias Stems for Appliqué" on pages 15–16 to cut, sew, and press the solid green 24" square into twenty-four ½" × 6" bias strip segments for the stems. Label these A.

3. Referring to "Making Templates" on page 11, use the patterns B, C, and D on page 57 to make templates. Trace the template

and cut pattern B (flower) 4 times from *each* of the 4 colors of fat quarters, adding a scant ¼"-wide seam allowance around the tracing line as you cut. Trace the templates and cut pattern C (large leaf) 16 times and pattern D (small leaf) 32 times from the remaining green solid fabric, once again adding a scant ¼"-wide seam allowance around the tracing line as you cut.

4. Using your preferred method, appliqué the pieces *in order*—4 C, 8 D, 4 A, and 4 B—to each light background block as indicated by the placement guidelines. Trim the blocks to measure 16½" × 16½".

◾ Making the Pieced Sashing

1. On a design wall or other flat surface, lay out eight 2½" print squares in a pleasing, random order. With right sides together, sew the squares to form a pieced strip. Press the seams carefully to one side *as you go*. Make six 8-square strips.

Make 6.

2. Repeat to lay out, sew, and press nineteen 2½" squares in a random pieced strip. Make three 19-square strips.

Make 3.

Assembling the Quilt

1. Alternate three 8-square sashing strips and 2 appliquéd blocks in a horizontal row as shown. With right sides together, pin and sew the sashing strips to the blocks, and then the sashed blocks into a row. Press all seams away from the blocks. Make 2 sashed block rows.

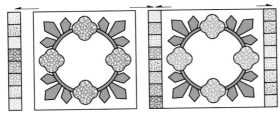

Make 2.

2. Refer to the quilt assembly diagram below to arrange the sashed blocks from step 1 and the long pieced sashing strips as shown.

Quilt Assembly Diagram

3. Carefully pin the rows together, matching the seams; then sew the rows together and press.
4. Pin and sew the $6\frac{1}{2}$" × $38\frac{1}{2}$" outer border strips to the sides of the quilt. Press the seams toward the border strips.
5. Divide one $6\frac{1}{2}$" × 42" outer border strip in half. Sew half to each of the remaining $6\frac{1}{2}$" × 42" border strips, and trim to make two $6\frac{1}{2}$" × $50\frac{1}{2}$" strips.
6. With right sides together, pin and sew the $6\frac{1}{2}$" × $50\frac{1}{2}$" outer border strips to the top and bottom edges of the quilt. Press the seams toward the border strips.

Making the Yo-Yos

1. Trace and cut the Yo-yo pattern on page 57 from your preferred template material. Use this template and the remaining assorted print scraps to trace and cut 16 fabric circles.
2. Use a double strand of sewing thread with a knotted end to take a running stitch around the perimeter of each fabric circle, folding over a scant $\frac{1}{4}$" as you go. Don't knot the finishing end of the thread.

3. Gently pull the thread to gather the circle right side out. Smooth it to center the bunched fabric, and tie off. Set the Yo-yo appliqué pieces aside for now.

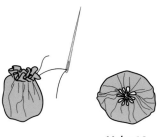

Make 16.

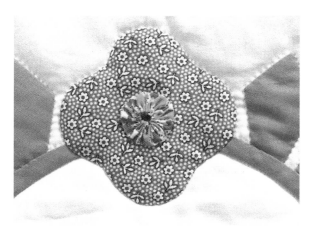

Detail of Yo-yo appliqué piece and flower

🌸 Finishing

1. Choose your own quilting design. Depending on your selection, follow the directions in "Marking the Quilting Lines" on page 19 to prepare the quilt top for quilting.

2. Divide the backing fabric crosswise into 2 equal panels of approximately 54" each. Remove the selvages and join the pieces to make a single large backing panel.

3. Referring to "Layering the Quilt" on page 19, center and layer the quilt top and the batting over the backing; baste.

4. Quilt as desired (see "Quilting Techniques" on pages 20–21).

5. Tack a Yo-yo appliqué piece of contrasting color, gathered side up, in the center of each appliquéd flower as shown in the color photo at top right.

6. Trim the batting and backing even with the edges of the quilt top. Refer to the instructions for bias-grain binding on page 22 to cut $2\frac{1}{4}$"-wide bias strips from the 24" square of binding fabric, for a total of approximately 210" of bias binding. Sew the binding strips to the quilt.

7. Make and attach a label to the quilt.

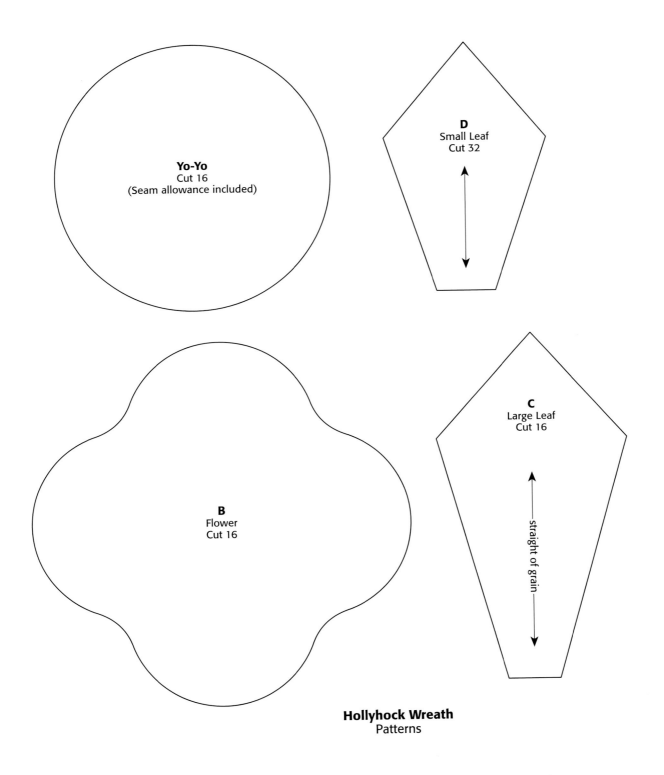

Yo-Yo
Cut 16
(Seam allowance included)

D
Small Leaf
Cut 32

B
Flower
Cut 16

C
Large Leaf
Cut 16

straight of grain

Hollyhock Wreath
Patterns

I was making a double wedding ring quilt when I came up with the idea that the same shapes would make a cute umbrella quilt. I made the ribbon handle because I wanted to know how it would look, and to speed up the block. I decided to keep it!

Cleo Nollette

Finished quilt size: 43" × 43"
Finished block size: 8½"

Materials

42"-wide fabric
1 fat eighth yellow '30s print for sashing
    corner squares
¼ yd. yellow '30s print for border corner
    squares
⅝ yd. *total* of assorted blue '30s prints for
    sashing
¼ yd. *each* of 4 different blue '30s prints
    for border
¾ yd. fabric for binding
⅞ yd. pale yellow tone-on-tone print or solid
    for block backgrounds
1 fat eighth *each* of 4 assorted blue '30s
    prints for umbrellas
1 fat eighth *each* of 3 assorted yellow '30s
    prints for umbrellas
2⅔ yds. fabric for backing
46" × 46" piece of batting
1¾ yds. blue grosgrain ribbon, ¼" wide
Scrap of template plastic

Cutting the Sashing, Border, and Binding

All measurements include ¼"-wide seam allowances.
From the yellow '30s print for sashing corner squares, cut:
    16 squares, each 2½" × 2½"
From the yellow '30s print for border corner squares, cut:
    4 squares, each 5" × 5"
From the assorted blue '30s prints for sashing, cut:
    A *total* of 24 strips, each 2½" × 9"
From *each* of the 4 blue '30s prints for the border, cut:
    1 strip, 5" × 34"
From the binding fabric, cut:
    1 square, 24" × 24", for bias binding

Cutting the Umbrella Blocks

Before you begin sewing, you'll need to make templates, trace them, and cut the pieces for the Umbrella blocks. Trace the pattern pieces A, C, and D on pages 64–65. Make a template for pattern piece X as well. (This will be used to double check for accuracy as you assemble the blocks.)

To make a template for piece B, fold an oversized sheet of white tracing paper in half. Align the fold with the fold line indicated on the pattern on page 65, and trace

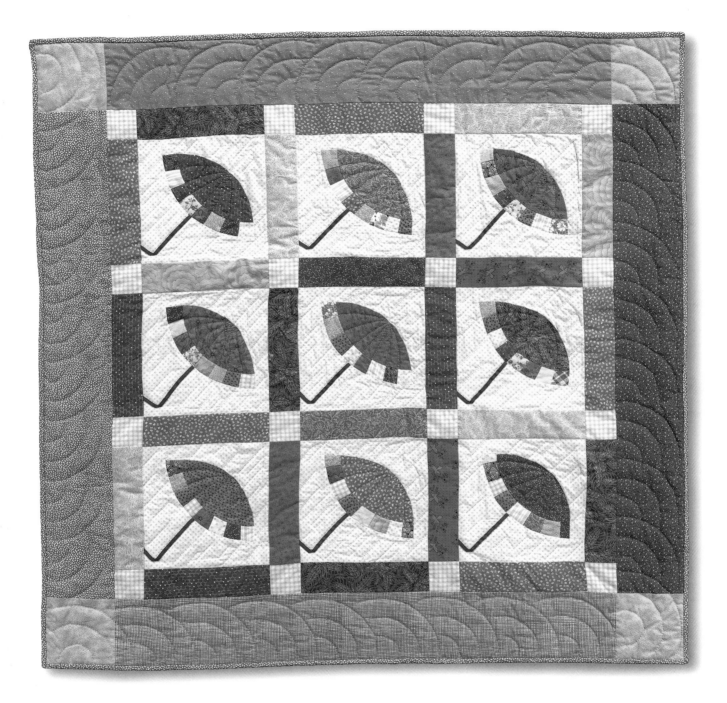

Summer in Seattle
By Cleo Nollette, 1999, Seattle, Washington

the pattern. Cut the paper directly on the traced lines. Unfold the tracing paper, and transfer the complete, symmetrical paper shape to the plastic template material. Cut out the template.

From the pale yellow tone-on-tone print or solid, cut:

　　9 A pieces for block backgrounds

　　9 B pieces for block backgrounds

From the 4 assorted blue '30s prints for the umbrellas, cut:

　　A *total* of 9 C pieces

From the 3 assorted yellow '30s prints for the umbrellas and the remaining yellow scraps, cut:

　　A *total* of 36 D pieces for the umbrella "trim"

From all remaining blue print scraps, cut:

　　A *total* of 36 D pieces for the umbrella "trim"

◣ Making the Blocks

You'll need a total of 9 Umbrella blocks for this quilt. Refer to "Machine Piecing" on pages 9–11 for general piecing techniques.

1. Gently press the 9 B background pieces in half. Do not stretch them out of shape.

2. Place a 6" length of $\frac{1}{4}$" grosgrain ribbon on the crease line of each B piece, folding the end to form a right angle approximately 1" from the corner. Machine stitch the ribbon in place with matching thread.

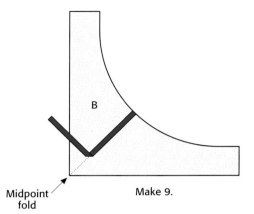

Midpoint fold   Make 9.

3. Arrange 4 blue and 4 yellow D pieces as shown, beginning with a blue piece and alternating colors. With right sides together, sew the pieces into an arc. Carefully press the seams toward the blue pieces *as you go*. Make 9 arcs.

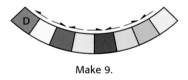

Make 9.

4. Use the X template to test the pieced arcs for accuracy. Trim or adjust the seams as necessary.

5. Gently finger press the C pieces to mark their centers. Place each C piece right sides together with a pieced arc. Pin at the ends, and match and pin the center of the arc to the center of C. Add additional pins, easing as necessary. Sew, then press the seam toward the C pieces. Make 9 Umbrella units.

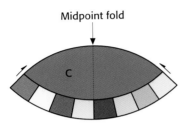

Midpoint fold

6. In a similar fashion, finger-press the A pieces to mark their centers. Place the curved edge of each A piece right sides together with the top edge of an Umbrella unit from step 5. Match and pin ends and centers, and ease as necessary. Sew, then press the seams toward the A piece.

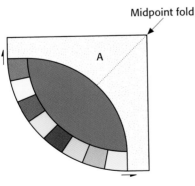

Midpoint fold

7. Place the curved edge of each Umbrella unit from step 6 right sides together with the curved edge of an embellished B piece from step 2. Match and pin ends and centers, using the umbrella handle as a guide. Use additional pins, easing as necessary. Sew, then press the seams toward the B piece. Make 9 blocks.

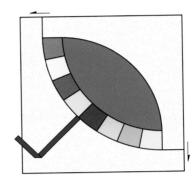

Assembling the Quilt Top

1. Alternate 4 sashing strips and 3 pieced blocks in a horizontal row as shown. With right sides together, pin and sew the sashing strips to the blocks, and then the sashed blocks to make a row. Press all seams away from the blocks. Make 3 rows.

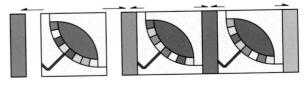

Make 3.

2. Alternate four 2½" yellow corner squares with three 2½" × 9" blue sashing strips as shown. Pin and sew the corner squares to the sashing strips to make a row. Press the seams away from the corner squares. Make 4 rows.

Make 4.

3. Refer to the quilt assembly diagram below and "Making Straight-Set Quilts" on page 16 to arrange the sashed blocks from step 1 and the pieced sashing strips as shown.

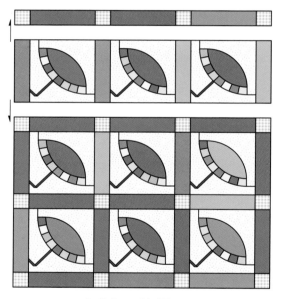

Quilt Assembly Diagram

4. Carefully pin the rows together, matching the seams; then sew the rows together and press.

5. Referring to "Adding Borders" on pages 17–18, pin and sew a 5" × 34" border strip to the sides of the quilt. Press the seams toward the border strips.

6. Referring to "Borders with Corner Squares" on page 18, sew a yellow 5" border corner square to each end of the remaining blue border strips. Pin and sew the strips to the top and bottom edges of the quilt. Press the seams toward the border strips.

Finishing

1. Choose your own quilting design. Depending on your selection, follow the directions in "Marking the Quilting Lines" on page 19 to prepare the quilt top for quilting.

2. Divide the backing fabric crosswise into 2 equal panels of approximately 48" each. Remove the selvages and join the pieces to make a single large backing panel.

3. Referring to "Layering the Quilt" on page 19, center and layer the quilt top and the batting over the backing; baste.

4. Quilt as desired (see "Quilting Techniques" on pages 20–21).

5. Trim the batting and backing even with the edges of the quilt top. Refer to the instructions for bias-grain binding on page 22 to cut 2¼"-wide bias strips from the 24" square of binding fabric, for a total of approximately 186" of bias binding. Sew the binding to the quilt.

6. Make and attach a label to the quilt.

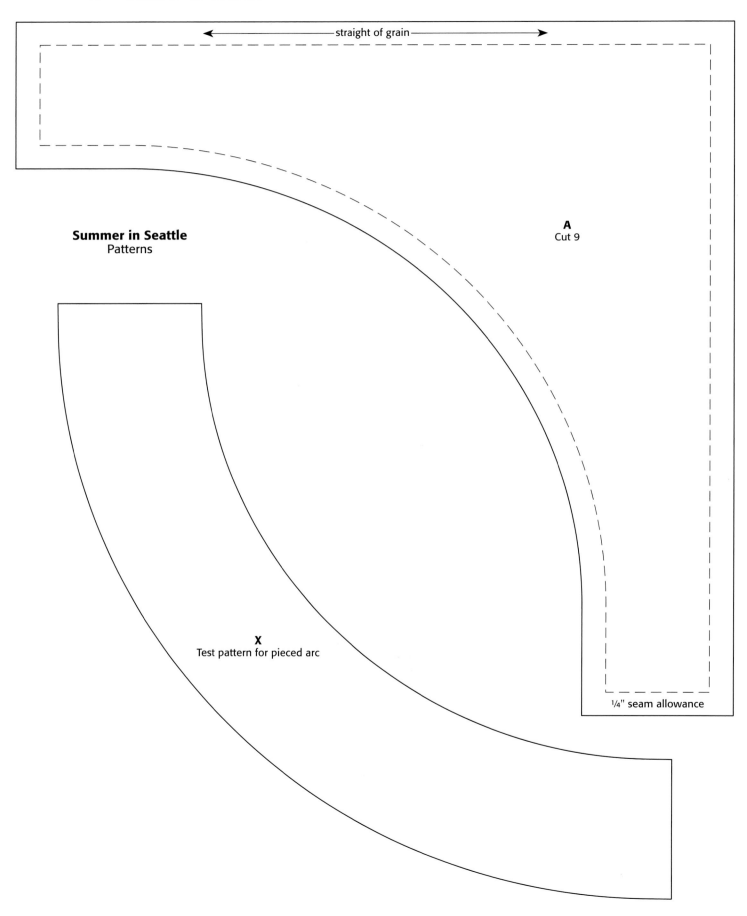

straight of grain

Summer in Seattle
Patterns

A
Cut 9

X
Test pattern for pieced arc

¼" seam allowance

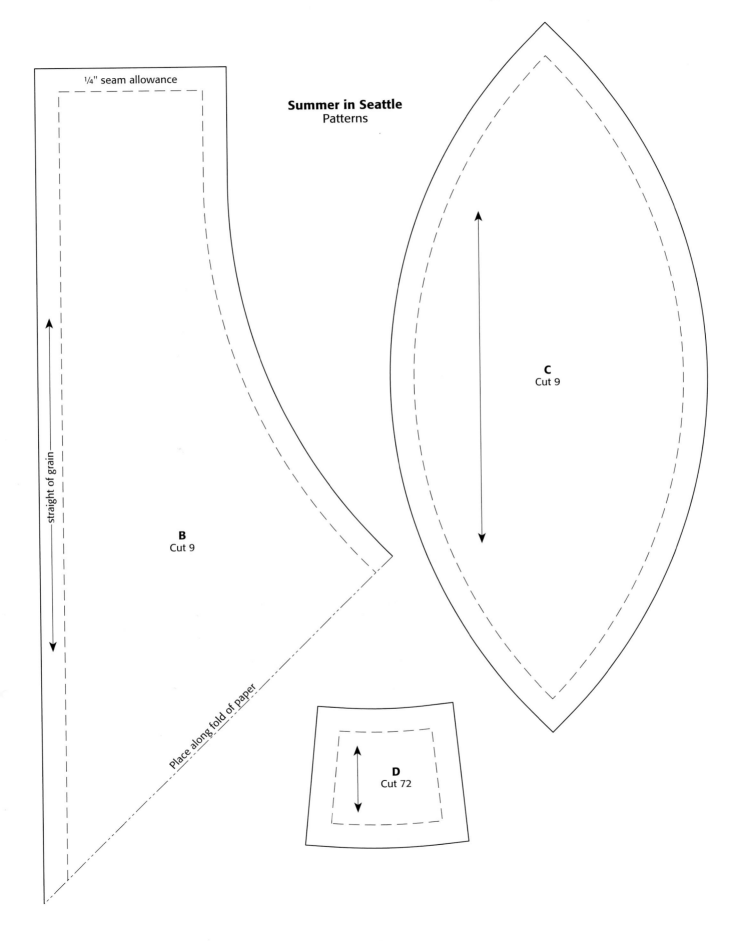

¼" seam allowance

Summer in Seattle
Patterns

straight of grain

B
Cut 9

Place along fold of paper

C
Cut 9

D
Cut 72

BARNEY AND FRIENDS

Playful, appliquéd cats were often featured in '30s quilts, especially in quilts for babies. A colorful mix of '30s prints adds to the charm of these stretching cats and creates a playful mood in this baby quilt.

I named this quilt for Barney, the last of a wonderful family of cats that we had for eighteen years. He was still alive when I made this quilt. That's why he's facing Truffles, his mother; Schatzie, his sister; and Blackie, his best buddy, who all preceded him to kitty heaven. He has since joined them. They may be gone, but they are not forgotten.

Ursula Reikes

> Finished quilt size: $39\frac{1}{2}$" × $39\frac{1}{2}$"
> Finished block size: 10"

◢ Materials

42"-wide fabric

$1\frac{1}{8}$ yds. white solid for appliqué backgrounds, blocks, and inner border

1 fat quarter *each* of 2 blue '30s prints for appliqué cat, blocks, and pieced border

1 fat quarter *each* of 2 green '30s prints for appliqué cat, blocks, and pieced border

1 fat quarter *each* of 4 pink '30s prints for appliqué cat, blocks, and pieced border

1 fat quarter *each* of 4 purple '30s prints for appliqué cat, blocks, and pieced border

1 fat quarter *each* of 4 yellow '30s prints for blocks and pieced border

$\frac{3}{8}$ yd. fabric for binding

$1\frac{1}{4}$ yds. fabric for backing

43" × 43" piece of batting

$\frac{1}{2}$ yd. of paper-backed fusible web

◢ Cutting

All measurements include $\frac{1}{4}$"-wide seam allowances.

From the white solid, cut:

   4 oversized squares, each $11\frac{1}{2}$" × $11\frac{1}{2}$", for appliqué background blocks

   25 squares, each $2\frac{1}{2}$" × $2\frac{1}{2}$", for pieced blocks

   2 strips, each 2" × $30\frac{1}{2}$", for inner side borders

   2 strips, each 2" × $33\frac{1}{2}$", for inner top and bottom borders

From the blue '30s prints, cut:

   A *total* of 9 squares, each $2\frac{1}{2}$" × $2\frac{1}{2}$", for pieced blocks

   A *total* of 5 rectangles, each $2\frac{1}{2}$" × $6\frac{1}{2}$", for pieced blocks

   A *total* of 2 squares, each $3\frac{1}{2}$" × $3\frac{1}{2}$", for pieced border

   A *total* of 4 squares, each $4\frac{1}{4}$" × $4\frac{1}{4}$", for pieced border

Barney and Friends
By Ursula Reikes, 1999, Ivins, Utah
Quilted by Alvina Nelson

From the green '30s prints, cut:

A *total* of 9 squares, each 2½" × 2½",
for pieced blocks

A *total* of 5 rectangles, each 2½" × 6½",
for pieced blocks

A *total* of 2 squares, each 3½" × 3½",
for pieced border

A *total* of 4 squares, each 4¼" × 4¼",
for pieced border

From the pink '30s prints, cut:

A *total* of 9 squares, each 2½" × 2½",
for pieced blocks

A *total* of 5 rectangles, each 2½" × 6½",
for pieced blocks

A *total* of 2 squares, each 3½" × 3½",
for pieced border

A *total* of 6 squares, each 4¼" × 4¼",
for pieced border

From the purple '30s prints, cut:

A *total* of 9 squares, each 2½" × 2½",
for pieced blocks

A *total* of 5 rectangles, each 2½" × 6½",
for pieced blocks

A *total* of 2 squares, each 3½" × 3½",
for pieced border

A *total* of 6 squares, each 4¼" × 4¼",
for pieced border

From the yellow '30s prints, cut:

A *total* of 20 squares, each 2½" × 2½",
for pieced blocks

A *total* of 20 squares, each 4¼" × 4¼",
for pieced border

From the binding fabric, cut:

5 strips, each 2½" × 42"

◆ Making the Appliqué Blocks

You'll need 4 appliqué Cat blocks for this quilt. Refer to "Basic Appliqué" starting on page 11 for general appliqué techniques. The instructions for "Barney and Friends" recommend the fusible appliqué method. Feel free to substitute traditional appliqué methods if you prefer. Just be sure to adapt the patterns, such as adding seam allowances when cutting the fabric shapes, as necessary.

1. Use the pattern on page 73 to make a template. Trace 4 cat shapes onto the paper side of the fusible web. Cut out the shapes, adding approximately ¼" beyond the drawn line.

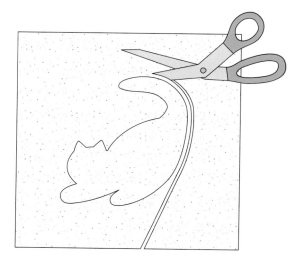

Ursula's Tip
To have one cat facing in the opposite direction (as shown in the sample), reverse the template before tracing one of the cats on the fusible web.

2. Fuse the paper shapes to the wrong side of remaining scraps of blue, green, pink, and purple fabrics. Cut out the shapes exactly on the drawn lines. Remove the paper and position each cat shape on the center of a white square. Follow the manufacturer's instructions to fuse the appliqué in place on the white background block.

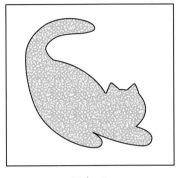

Make 4.

3. Stitch around each cat shape with a blanket stitch. You can do this by hand or by machine. Trim the appliquéd blocks to measure $10\frac{1}{2}$" × $10\frac{1}{2}$".

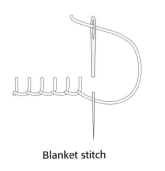

Blanket stitch

4. Draw a diagonal line from corner to corner on the wrong side of four $2\frac{1}{2}$" blue, green, pink, and purple squares. With right sides together, align a different colored print square on each corner of an appliquéd square. Stitch on the drawn line and trim away the excess, leaving a $\frac{1}{4}$" seam allowance. Press the triangle toward the corner. Repeat for all 4 appliquéd blocks.

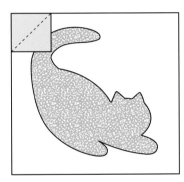

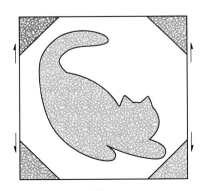

Make 4.

◤ Making the Pieced Blocks

1. Arrange five 2½" white squares, and 1 each of the 2½" blue, green, pink, and purple squares as shown to make a nine-patch unit. If needed, refer to the photo on page 67 for guidance in arranging the squares.

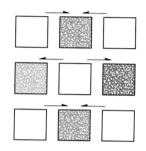

2. With right sides together, pin and sew the squares together into rows. Press the seams as shown above.

3. Carefully pin the rows together, matching the seams; then sew the rows together and press. Make 5 of these nine-patch units.

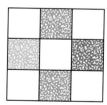

Make 5.

4. Arrange four 2½" yellow squares, 1 each of the 2½" × 6½" blue, green, pink, and purple rectangles, and a nine-patch unit as shown. Sew the rectangle between the 2 yellow squares to complete rows 1 and 3, and the nine-patch unit between the 2 rectangles to complete row 2. Press all seams toward the rectangles.

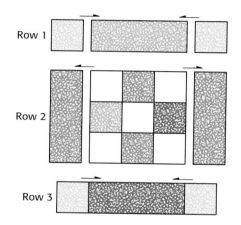

5. Carefully pin the rows together, matching the seams; then sew the rows together and press. Repeat to complete 5 blocks.

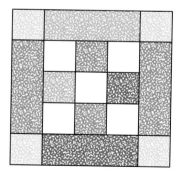

Make 5.

🔷 Assembling the Quilt Top

1. Refer to the quilt assembly diagram below and "Making Straight-Set Quilts" on page 16 to arrange alternating pieced and appliquéd blocks in 3 rows of 3 blocks each. Rows 1 and 3 begin with pieced blocks, and row 2 begins with an appliquéd block.

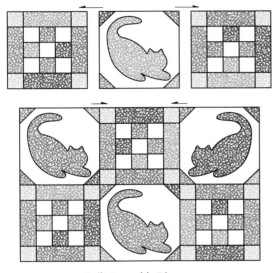

Quilt Assembly Diagram

2. Pin and sew the blocks together into rows. Press the seams toward the pieced blocks.

3. Carefully pin the rows together, matching the seams; then sew the rows together and press.

4. Referring to "Adding Borders" on pages 17–18, pin and sew the 2" × 30½" inner border strips to the sides of the quilt. Press the seams toward the border strips. Repeat to pin and sew the 2" × 33½" inner border strips to the top and bottom edges of the quilt. Press.

🔷 Making and Adding the Pieced Border

1. Refer to "Cut-and-Pieced Squares" on page 10. Pair each 4¼" yellow square with a 4¼" blue, green, pink, or purple square to make a total of 40 half-square triangle units. Press the seams away from the yellow triangles. Use a Bias Square Ruler to trim all sides of the units to 3½" × 3½".

> *Ursula's Tip*
> *Sewing triangle units that are larger than needed, and then trimming them to the required size, results in more accurately sized finished units.*

2. Arrange 5 half-square triangle units on opposite sides of a 3½" print square as shown. Be sure that the yellow triangles are turned correctly on either side of the square. Pin, sew, and press. Make 4 pieced borders.

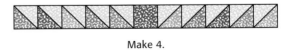

Make 4.

3. Pin and sew pieced borders to the sides of the quilt top, orienting the yellow triangles away from the center. Refer to the color photo on page 67 for guidance. Press the seams away from the white inner border.

4. Referring to "Borders with Corner Squares" on page 18, add a 3½" print square to each end of the remaining pieced borders. Press the seams away from the corner squares. Carefully pin the borders to the top and bottom edges of the quilt top, matching the seams; then sew the pieced borders to the top and bottom edges of the quilt and press.

Finishing

1. Choose your own quilting design. Depending on your selection, you may need to mark the quilt top with the design. If so, refer to the steps in "Marking the Quilting Lines" on page 19.

2. Referring to "Layering the Quilt" on page 19, center and layer the quilt top and the batting over the backing; baste.

3. Quilt as desired (see "Quilting Techniques" on pages 20–21).

4. Trim the batting and backing even with the edges of the quilt top. Referring to "Binding" on pages 22–23, use the 2½" × 42" strips to make the binding; then sew the binding to the quilt.

5. Make and attach a label to your quilt.

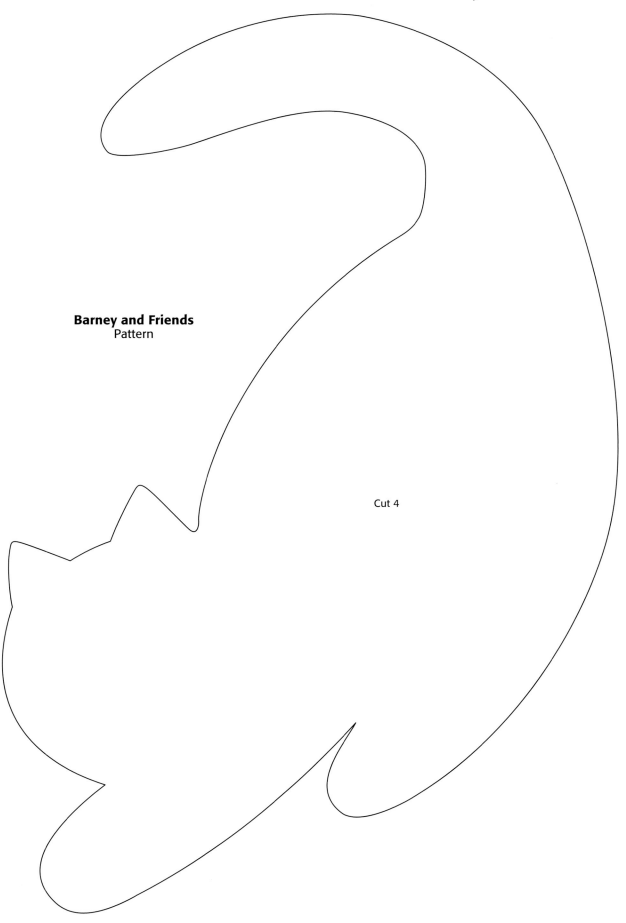

Barney and Friends
Pattern

Cut 4

SCRAPPY GARDEN PATH

This quilt was inspired by a photo found in an old book. My friend Sarah Achterhof shared it with me. I sized down the block measurement as well as the overall size of the quilt to better suit the small scale of the typical '30s print. Most of the fabrics in my quilt are reproductions. The one exception is the purple print, which belonged to my grandmother. It fit in perfectly!

Retta Warehime

Finished quilt size: $52\frac{1}{2}$" $\times$ $67\frac{1}{2}$"

Materials

42"-wide fabric

$1\frac{2}{3}$ yds. muslin for center squares, inner border, and outer border

17 fat quarters of assorted '30s solids and prints for sashing and pieced border*

$\frac{1}{2}$ yd. fabric for binding**

4 yds. fabric for backing

56" $\times$ 71" piece of batting

* May also be thirty-four $\frac{1}{8}$ yds. or assorted scraps to total approximately $3\frac{1}{4}$ yds.
** May be scraps to total a long continuous strip— $2\frac{1}{2}$" $\times$ 250".

Cutting

All measurements include $\frac{1}{4}$"-wide seam allowances.

From the muslin, cut:

88 squares, each $3\frac{1}{2}$" $\times$ $3\frac{1}{2}$", for center squares

5 strips, each $1\frac{1}{2}$" $\times$ 42", for inner borders

6 strips, each $3\frac{1}{2}$" $\times$ 42", for outer borders

From the assorted '30s prints and solids, cut:

143 strips, each $1\frac{1}{2}$" $\times$ 22", for sashing and pieced border

From binding fabric, cut:

6 strips, each $2\frac{1}{2}$" $\times$ 42"*

*$2\frac{1}{2}$" $\times$ 250" total for scrappy binding.

Piecing the Sashing

There is no block in "Scrappy Garden Path." The entire quilt is composed of 3" finished muslin squares separated by sashing—or "paths"—and borders pieced from 1,812 squares, each with a 1" $\times$ 1" finished size! Don't let the numbers scare you. The sashing and borders are pieced as strip sets that are cut apart and easily (and accurately) reassembled.

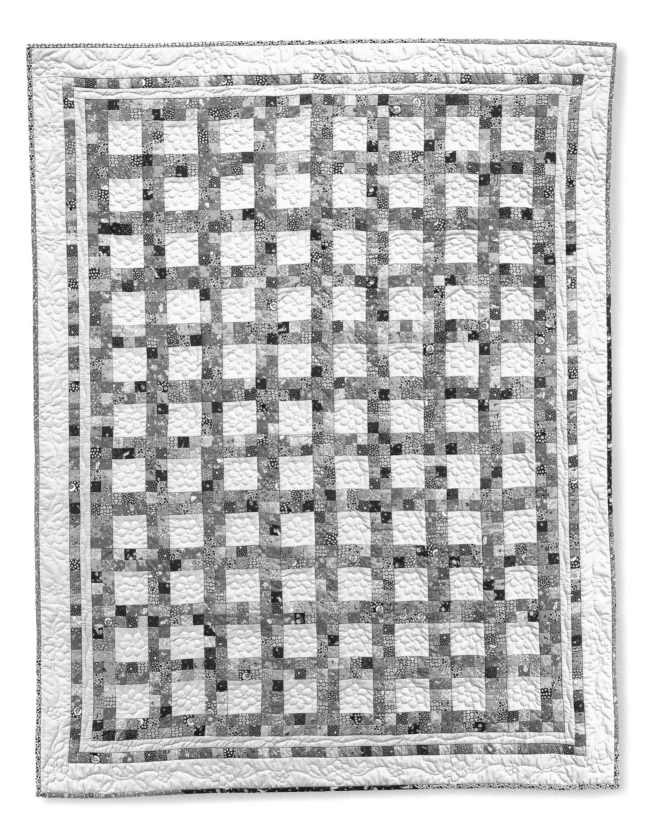

Scrappy Garden Path
By Retta Warehime, 1999, Kennewick, Washington

1. With right sides together and long raw edges aligned, sew 3 assorted 1½" × 22" strips together to make a strip set. Press the seams to one side. The strip set should measure 3½" × 22" when sewn and pressed. Make 31 strip sets.

2. Crosscut the strip sets into 392 segments that are 1½" wide. Use 390 of the segments for the sashing and 2 for the pieced border. Label these 3-strip segments A.

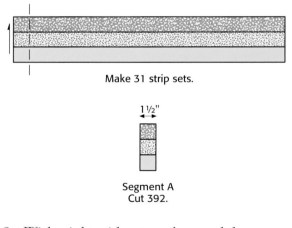

Make 31 strip sets.

1½"

Segment A
Cut 392.

3. With right sides together and long raw edges aligned, sew 2 assorted 1½" × 22" strips together to make a strip set. Press the seams to one side. The strip set should measure 2½" × 22" when sewn and pressed. Make 25 strip sets.

4. Crosscut the strip sets into 308 segments that measure 1½" wide. Use 216 for the sashing and 92 for the pieced borders. Label these 2-strip segments B.

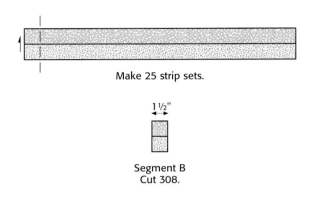

Make 25 strip sets.

1½"

Segment B
Cut 308.

5. With right sides together and long raw edges aligned, sew 2 A segments together to make a 6-square "path." Be sure to pin carefully to match the seams. Press the seam to one side. Make 195. Label these 6-square units C.

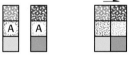

Unit C
Make 195.

6. With right sides together and long raw edges aligned, sew 2 B segments together to make a 4-square "path." Be sure to pin carefully to match the seams. Press the seam. Make 108. Label these 4-square units D.

Unit D
Make 108.

7. Arrange 28 B segments and 1 A segment end to end as shown. Pin and sew the segments together to make a 59-square side pieced border. Press the seams to one side. Make 2.

Side pieced borders
Make 2.

8. Arrange 23 B segments end to end as shown. Pin and sew the segments together to make a 46-square top pieced border. Press the seams to one side. Repeat to make a bottom pieced border.

Top and bottom pieced borders
Make 2.

9. Alternate 8 C units and 9 D units end to end as shown, beginning with a D unit. Pin and sew the units, and press the seams toward the C units. Make 12 rows and label them X.

Row X
Make 12.

10. Alternate 9 C units and eight 3½" muslin squares as shown, beginning with a C unit. Press and sew the units and squares to make a row, and press the seams toward the C units. Make 11 rows and label them Y.

Row Y
Make 11.

◢ Assembling the Quilt

1. Refer to the quilt assembly diagram below and "Making Straight-Set Quilts" on page 16 to arrange alternating X and Y rows as shown. Begin and end with an X row.

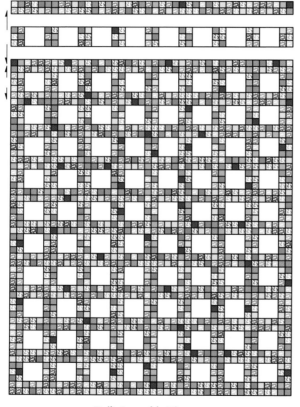

Quilt Assembly Diagram

2. Carefully pin the rows together, matching the seams; then sew the rows together. Press toward row X.

3. Sew the $1\frac{1}{2}" \times 42"$ muslin inner border strips end to end to make one long continuous strip. Cut the strip into two $1\frac{1}{2}" \times 44\frac{1}{2}"$ strips for the top and bottom inner borders, and two $1\frac{1}{2}" \times 57\frac{1}{2}"$ strips for the side inner borders.

Retta's Tip

Remember that the pieced borders must fit the cut size of the muslin border strips! Because of the many seam allowances involved, you may need to make some adjustments.

4. Referring to "Adding Borders" on pages 17–18, pin and sew the $1\frac{1}{2}" \times 57\frac{1}{2}"$ inner border strips to the sides of the quilt. Press the seams toward the inner border strips. Repeat to sew the $1\frac{1}{2}" \times 44\frac{1}{2}"$ inner border strips to the top and bottom edges of the quilt. Press the seams toward the inner border strips.

5. Sew the 59-square side pieced borders to the sides of the quilt. Press the seams away from the pieced borders. Repeat to add the 46-square pieced borders to the top and bottom edges of the quilt.

6. Sew the $3\frac{1}{2}" \times 42"$ muslin outer border strips end to end to make one long continuous strip. Cut the strip into two $3\frac{1}{2}" \times 61\frac{1}{2}"$ strips for the side outer borders, and two $3\frac{1}{2}" \times 52\frac{1}{2}"$ strips for the top and bottom borders.

7. Pin and sew the $3\frac{1}{2}" \times 61\frac{1}{2}"$ outer border strips to the sides of the quilt. Press the seams toward the outer border strips. Repeat to sew the $3\frac{1}{2}" \times 52\frac{1}{2}"$ outer border strips to the top and bottom edges of the quilt. Press the seams toward the outer border strips.

◆ Finishing

1. Choose your own quilting design. Depending on your selection, follow the directions in "Marking the Quilting Lines" on page 19 to prepare the quilt top for quilting.

2. Divide the backing fabric crosswise into 2 equal panels of approximately 72" each. Remove the selvages and join the pieces to make a single large backing panel.

3. Referring to "Layering the Quilt" on page 19, center and layer the quilt top and the batting over the backing; baste.

4. Quilt as desired (see "Quilting Techniques" on pages 20–21).

5. Trim the batting and backing even with the edges of the quilt top. Referring to "Binding" on pages 22–23, use the 2½" × 42" strips to make the binding; then sew the binding to the quilt.

6. Make and attach a label to the finished quilt.

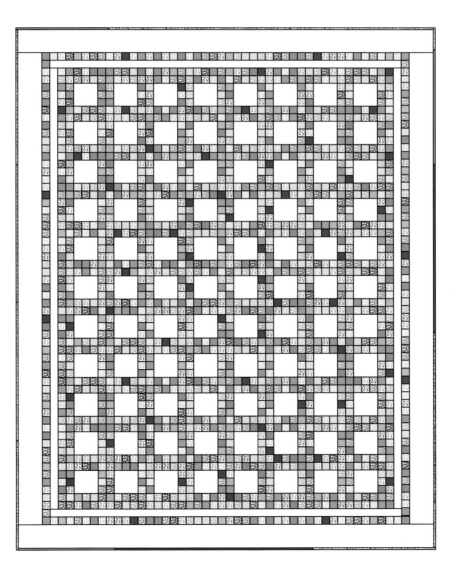

DOROTHY'S GARDEN GIRLS

orothy's Garden Girls is one of those wonderful mother-daughter projects. Dorothy Everett Whitelaw, my mother, began the quilt in 1933, and I completed it in 1989—more than 55 years later!

As my mother began sorting through a lifetime's accumulation of treasures in our family home, she passed along to me ten charming Garden Girl blocks that she had made from her dress fabrics when she was a young teen. This was quite a surprise and thrill to me (an avid sewer and quilter from a young age) because she had always told me that she didn't care for sewing and that threading a needle made her nervous. My grandmother was an accomplished seamstress and I had assumed that the talent had skipped a generation. I was pleased to see that my mother had some sewing talent and skill also. I began planning a quilt that I could make out of her delightful blocks and give to her on her upcoming seventieth birthday. Since I couldn't figure out how to set ten blocks into a quilt design, I used nine on the front and used the tenth on the back as a label. Sometime later she handed me two additional blocks, saying that she must have made twelve after all. With these two extra blocks, I made two doll quilts, which are shown below. Project directions for these doll quilts begin on page 87.

Joan Whitelaw Hanson

Finished quilt size: 43" × 47½"
Finished block size: 6½" × 8"

Dorothy's Garden Girls
Blocks by Dorothy Everett Whitelaw, 1933
Assembled and quilted by Joan Whitelaw Hanson, 1989, Seattle, Washington

◼ Materials

42"-wide fabric

⅔ yd. light fabric for appliqué background blocks

1⅛ yds. blue solid for sashing, setting squares, and binding

1¼ yds. blue '30s print for sashing, setting squares, and border

Assorted scraps of '30s prints for appliqué dresses and hats*

2⅞ yds. fabric for backing

44" × 49" piece of batting

Embroidery floss in black and assorted floral colors

*Total approximately 1 yd.

◼ Cutting

All measurements include ¼"-wide seam allowances.

From the light fabric, cut:

　9 oversized rectangles, each 8" × 9½", for appliqué backgrounds

From the blue solid fabric, cut:

　12 strips, each 1½" × 42", for sashing and setting squares

　2 strips, each 2¼" × 42", for sashing and setting squares

　5 strips, each 2½" × 42", for binding

From the blue '30s print fabric, cut:

　6 strips, each 2¼" × 42", for sashing and setting squares

　6 strips, each 1½" × 42", for sashing and setting squares

　4 strips, each 4½" × 42", for outer borders

◼ Making the Appliqué Blocks

You'll need 9 appliqué blocks for this quilt. Refer to "Basic Appliqué" starting on page 11 for general appliqué techniques. Choose the appliqué method you prefer and follow the instructions appropriate to that method.

There are only 2 pieces to appliqué for each block: a matching print hat and dress. All the little details—shoes and socks, hatband, ribbon, flowers, and petticoat—are added with embroidery stitches.

1. Refer to "Marking and Cutting Fabric" on page 11 and use the appliqué and embroidery placement diagram on page 95 to prepare and mark the 8" × 9½" light background blocks for appliqué. If you'd like, reverse the Garden Girl pattern on 3 blocks as shown in the color photo on page 81.

2. Referring to "Making Templates" on page 11, use the Garden Girl patterns on page 95 to make the templates. Trace and cut 1 piece A (dress) and 1 piece B (hat) from the same '30s print, adding a scant ¼"-wide seam allowance around the traced line as you cut. Repeat 8 more times with different fabrics, cutting a total of 9 of piece A and 9 of piece B. Make sure to use matching pieces A and B for each block. Reverse the templates for 3 of each piece if you want 3 reversed blocks.

3. Using your preferred method, appliqué piece A and its matching piece B to each light background block. Trim the appliquéd blocks to measure 7" × 8½".

4. Use the black embroidery thread to outline the hat, dress, petticoat, arm, socks, and shoes. Add a hatband, bow, and creases in the skirt as shown in the appliqué and embroidery placement diagram on page 95 and the photo below.

5. Use the floral colored embroidery floss to outline the nosegays and add flowers or any other embellishments you wish.

Making the Pieced Sashing and Setting Squares

1. With right sides together and raw edges aligned, stitch a $1\frac{1}{2}" \times 42"$ blue solid strip to each long side of a $2\frac{1}{4}" \times 42"$ blue print strip to make a strip set. Press the seams toward the solid strips. Make 6 strip sets. Each strip set should measure $4\frac{1}{4}" \times 42"$ when sewn and pressed.

Detail of appliqué block

2. Crosscut the strip sets into twelve 7" segments and twelve 8½" segments. Label the 7"-wide segments A and the 8½"-wide segments B.

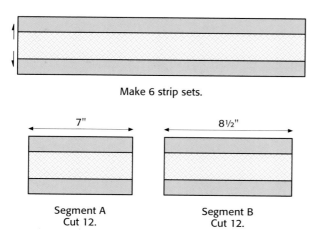

Make 6 strip sets.

|← 7" →| |← 8½" →|

Segment A
Cut 12.

Segment B
Cut 12.

3. With right sides together and raw edges aligned, stitch a 1½" × 42" blue print strip to each long side of a 2¼" × 42" blue solid strip to make a strip set. Press the seams toward the solid strip. Make 2 strip sets. Each strip set should measure 4¼" × 42" when sewn and pressed.

4. Crosscut the strip sets into thirty-two 1½"-wide segments. Label these segments C.

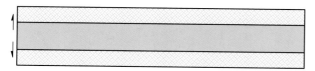

Make 2 strip sets.

1½"

Segment C
Cut 32.

5. Use the leftover strip sets from step 1 to cut sixteen 2¼"-wide segments. Label these segments D.

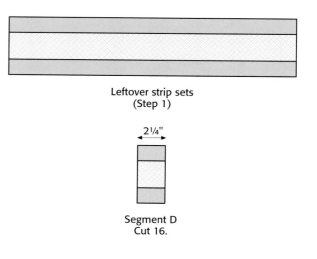

Leftover strip sets
(Step 1)

2¼"

Segment D
Cut 16.

6. Pin and sew a C segment to opposite sides of each D segment as shown. Press the seams toward the D segment. Make a total of 16 pieced setting squares.

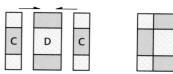

C   D   C

Make 16.

Assembling the Quilt

1. Alternate 4 B sashing strip segments and 3 appliquéd blocks in a horizontal row as shown. (If you've made 3 reverse Garden Girls blocks, place them first in each row.) Pin and sew the sashing strips to the blocks, and then the sashed blocks together to make a row. Press all seams away from the blocks. Make 3 rows.

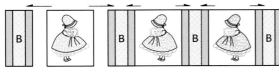

Make 3 rows.

2. Alternate 4 pieced setting squares with 3 A sashing strip segments as shown. Pin and sew the squares to the sashing strips to make a row. Press the seams away from the pieced setting squares. Make 4 rows.

Make 4 rows.

3. Refer to the quilt assembly diagram below and "Making Straight-Set Quilts" on page 16 to arrange the sashed blocks from step 1 and the pieced sashing strips as shown.

Quilt Assembly Diagram

4. Pin the rows together, matching the seams; then sew the rows together. Press as indicated by the arrows.

5. Sew the blue print 4½" × 42" outer border strips end to end to make one long continuous strip. Cut the strip into two 4½" × 39½" strips for the side outer borders, and two 4½" × 43" strips for the top and bottom borders.

6. Referring to "Adding Borders" on pages 17–18, pin and sew the 4½" × 39½" outer border strips to the sides of the quilt. Press the seams toward the border strips. Repeat to sew the 4½" × 43" outer border strips to the top and bottom edges of the quilt. Press the seams toward the border strips.

Finishing

1. Choose your own quilting design. Depending on your selection, follow the directions in "Marking the Quilting Lines" on page 19 to prepare the quilt top for quilting.

2. Divide the backing fabric crosswise into 2 panels of approximately 51" each. Remove the selvages and join the pieces to make a single large backing panel.

3. Referring to "Layering the Quilt" on page 19, center and layer the quilt top and the batting over the backing; baste.

4. Quilt as desired (see "Quilting Techniques" on pages 20–21).

5. Trim the batting and backing even with the edges of the quilt top. Referring to "Binding" on pages 22–23, use the 2½" × 42" strips to make the binding and sew the binding to the quilt.

6. Make and attach a label to the quilt.

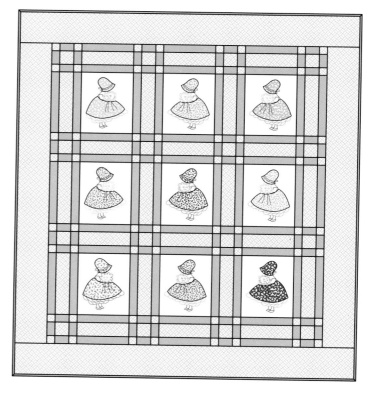

GARDEN GIRL
DOLL QUILT 1

Finished quilt size: $21\frac{1}{4}" \times 21\frac{1}{4}"$
Finished Garden Girl block size: $8" \times 8"$
Finished Pinwheel block size: $3" \times 3"$

◤ Materials

42"-wide fabric

$\frac{3}{8}$ yd. light fabric for appliqué background
   block and pieced blocks
$\frac{1}{2}$ yd. total of assorted '30s prints for
   appliqué dress, hat, pieced blocks, and
   binding
$\frac{1}{8}$ yd. '30s mint green solid for first border
$\frac{1}{3}$ yd. light blue solid for second and fourth
   borders
$\frac{3}{4}$ yd. for backing
$25" \times 25"$ piece of batting
Embroidery floss in black and assorted
   floral colors

◤ Cutting

*All measurements include $\frac{1}{4}"$-wide seam
allowances.*

From the light fabric, cut:
   1 oversized square, $9\frac{1}{2}" \times 9\frac{1}{2}"$, for
      appliqué background
   40 squares, each $2\frac{3}{8}" \times 2\frac{3}{8}"$, for pieced
      border
From the assorted '30s prints, cut:
   A total of 40 squares, each $2\frac{3}{8}" \times 2\frac{3}{8}"$,
      for pieced border
   A total of 7 strips, each $2\frac{1}{2}" \times 14"$, for
      binding
From the '30s mint green solid, cut:
   2 strips, each $1" \times 8\frac{1}{2}"$, for first side
      borders
   2 strips, each $1" \times 9\frac{1}{2}"$, for first top and
      bottom borders
From the light blue solid, cut:
   2 strips, each $2" \times 9\frac{1}{2}"$, for second side
      borders
   2 strips, each $2" \times 12\frac{1}{2}"$, for second top
      and bottom borders
   2 strips, each $2" \times 18\frac{1}{2}"$, for fourth side
      borders
   2 strips, each $2" \times 21\frac{1}{2}"$, for fourth top
      and bottom borders

Making the Appliqué Block

You'll need 1 appliqué block for this quilt. Refer to "Making the Appliqué Blocks" on pages 82–83 in "Dorothy's Garden Girls," for directions to make this block. Use the Garden Girl patterns on page 95 to make the templates. Use the 9" × 9" light fabric for the background, and trim the block after appliquéing and embroidering to measure 8½" × 8½".

Make 1.

Making the Pieced Blocks for Third Border

1. Refer to "Cut-and-Pieced Squares" on page 10. Pair each 2⅜" light fabric square with a 2⅜" print square to make a total of 80 half-square triangle units. Press the seams away from the light triangles.

2. Arrange 4 different-colored, half-square triangle units as shown. Be sure the '30s print triangles are turned correctly to create the pinwheel.

3. With right sides together, pin and sew the squares together into rows. Press the seams in opposite directions.

4. Carefully pin the rows together, matching the seams; then sew the rows together and press. Make 20 Pinwheel blocks.

Make 20.

5. Arrange 4 Pinwheel blocks in a vertical row. With right sides together and carefully matching the center seams, pin and sew the blocks together to make a pieced side border. Make 2.

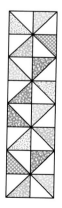

Make 2.

6. Arrange 6 Pinwheel blocks in a horizontal row. With right sides together and carefully matching the center seams, pin and sew the blocks together to make the top pieced border. Repeat to make the bottom pieced border.

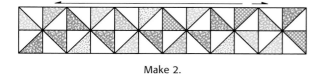

Make 2.

Assembling the Quilt Top

1. Pin and sew the 1" × 8½" strips for the first border to the sides of the appliquéd square. Press the seams toward the border strips. Repeat to sew the 1" × 9½" strips for the first border to the top and bottom edges of the quilt.

2. Pin and sew the 2" × 9½" strips for the second border to the sides of the framed appliqué block. Press the seams toward the border strips. Repeat to sew the 2" × 12½" strips for the second border to the top and bottom edges.

3. Pin and sew the 4-block, vertical pieced borders to the sides of the quilt. Press the seams toward the light blue border. Repeat to sew the 6-block, horizontal pieced borders to the top and bottom edges of the quilt.

Quilt Assembly Diagram

4. Pin and sew the 2" × 18½" light blue strips for the fourth border to the sides of the quilt. Press the seams toward the border strips. Repeat to sew the 2" × 21½" light blue strips for the fourth border to the top and bottom edges of the quilt.

◆ Finishing

1. Choose your own quilting design. Depending on your selection, follow the directions in "Marking the Quilting Lines" on page 19 to prepare the quilt top for quilting.

2. Referring to "Layering the Quilt" on page 19, center and layer the quilt top and the batting over the backing; baste.

3. Quilt as desired (see "Quilting Techniques" on pages 20–21).

4. Trim the batting and backing even with the edges of the quilt top. Referring to "Binding" on pages 22–23, join the 2½" × 14" '30s print strips end to end to make one continuous strip for the binding. Sew the binding to the quilt.

5. Make and attach a label to the finished quilt.

GARDEN GIRL DOLL QUILT 2

Finished quilt size: $21\frac{1}{4}$" × $21\frac{1}{4}$"
Finished block size: 8" × 8"

Materials

42"-wide fabric

$\frac{1}{2}$ yd. light fabric for appliqué background block and pieced outer border

$\frac{1}{2}$ yd. total of assorted '30s prints for appliqué dress, hat, and pieced outer border

$\frac{1}{8}$ yd. '30s mint green solid for inner border

$\frac{1}{3}$ yd. light blue solid for middle border and binding

$\frac{3}{4}$ yd. for backing

25" × 25" piece of batting

Embroidery floss in black and assorted floral colors

Cutting

All measurements include $\frac{1}{4}$"-wide seam allowances.

From the light fabric, cut:
  1 oversized square, $9\frac{1}{2}$" × $9\frac{1}{2}$", for appliqué background
  4 rectangles, each $1\frac{1}{4}$" × 2", for pieced outer border
  18 strips, each $1\frac{1}{4}$" × 9", for pieced outer border
  19 strips, each 2" × 6", for pieced outer border

From the assorted '30s prints, cut:
  A *total* of 15 strips, each 2" × 9", for pieced outer border
  A *total* of 21 strips, each $1\frac{1}{4}$" × 6", for pieced outer border
  A *total* of 6 squares, each $1\frac{1}{4}$" × $1\frac{1}{4}$", for pieced outer border

From the '30s mint green solid, cut:
  2 strips, each 1" × $8\frac{1}{2}$", for inner side borders
  2 strips, each 1" × $9\frac{1}{2}$", for inner top and bottom borders

From the light blue solid, cut:
  2 strips, each $1\frac{1}{4}$" × $9\frac{1}{2}$", for middle side borders
  2 strips, each $1\frac{1}{4}$" × 11", for middle top and bottom borders
  3 strips, each $2\frac{1}{2}$" × 42", for binding.

◆ Making the Appliqué Block

You'll need 1 appliqué block for this quilt. Refer to "Making the Appliqué Blocks" on pages 82–83 in "Dorothy's Garden Girls" for directions to make this block. Use the Garden Girl patterns on page 95 to make the templates. Use the 9½" × 9½" light fabric for the background and trim the block after appliquéing and embroidering to measure 8½" × 8½".

Make 1.

◆ Making the Pieced Outer Border

1. Alternate three 1¼" × 9" light strips and two 2" × 9" print strips, beginning and ending with a light strip to make Strip Set A. With right sides together and raw edges aligned, stitch the strips together. Press the seams toward the print strips. Each strip set should measure 5¾" × 9" when sewn and pressed. Make 3 strip sets.

2. Crosscut the 3 strip sets into a total of 10 segments, each 2" wide. Label these segments A units.

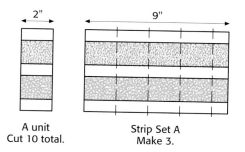

A unit
Cut 10 total.

Strip Set A
Make 3.

3. Alternate three 1¼" × 9" light strips and three 2" × 9" print strips to make Strip Set B. With right sides together and raw edges aligned, stitch the strips together. Press the seams toward the print strips. Each strip set should measure 7¼" × 9" when sewn and pressed. Make 3 strip sets.

4. Crosscut the 3 strip sets into a total of 12 segments, each 2" wide. Label these segments B units.

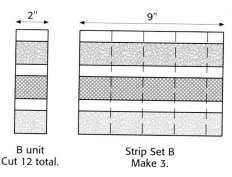

B unit
Cut 12 total.

Strip Set B
Make 3.

5. Alternate three 1¼" × 6" print strips and two 2" × 6" light strips, beginning and ending with a print strip to make Strip Set C. With right sides together and raw edges aligned, stitch the strips together. Press the seams toward the print strips. Each strip set should measure 5¾" × 6" when sewn and pressed. Make 2 strip sets.

6. Crosscut the 2 strip sets into a total of 8 segments, each 1¼" wide. Label these segments C units.

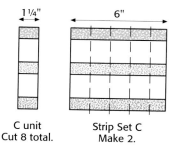

C unit
Cut 8 total.

Strip Set C
Make 2.

7. Alternate three 1¼" × 6" print strips and three 2" × 6" light strips to make Strip Set D. With right sides together and raw edges aligned, stitch the strips together. Press the seams toward the print strips. Each strip set should measure 7¼" × 6" when sewn and pressed. Make 5 strip sets.

8. Crosscut the 5 strip sets into a total of 18 segments, each 1¼" wide. Label these segments D units.

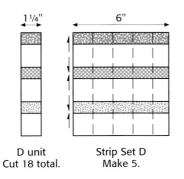

D unit
Cut 18 total.

Strip Set D
Make 5.

🔺 Assembling the Quilt Top

1. Pin and sew the 1" × 8½" inner border strips to the sides of the appliquéd square. Press the seams toward the border strips. Repeat to sew the 1" × 9½" inner border strips to the top and bottom edges of the quilt.

2. Pin and sew the 1¼" × 9½" middle border strips to the sides of the appliquéd square. Press the seams toward the light blue border strips. Repeat to sew the 1¼" × 11" middle border strips to the top and bottom edges of the quilt.

3. Alternate 5 A units and 4 C units, beginning and ending with an A unit as shown. Carefully matching the seams, pin and sew the units together to make a side pieced border. Press the seams toward the C units. Make 2.

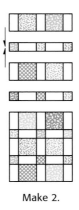

Make 2.

4. Arrange 3 B units in a horizontal row as shown. Pin and sew the units together. Sew a 1¼" × 2" light rectangle to the right-hand end of the row to complete the row. Press the seams toward the print squares. Make 4.

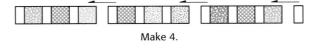

Make 4.

5. Arrange 3 D units in a horizontal row as shown. Pin and sew the units together. Sew a 1¼" × 1¼" '30s print square to the right-hand end of the row to complete the row. Press the seams toward the print squares. Make 6.

Make 6.

6. Alternate 2 rows of B units and 3 rows of D units, beginning and ending with a row of D units as shown. Carefully matching the seams, pin and sew the rows together to make the top pieced border. Press the seams toward the rows of D units. Repeat to make the bottom pieced border.

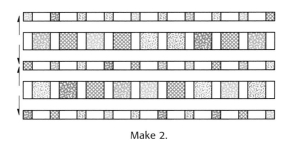

Make 2.

7. Pin and sew the pieced side borders to the sides of the framed appliqué block. Press the seams toward the center of the quilt. Repeat to sew the pieced top and bottom borders to the top and bottom edges of the quilt.

Quilt Assembly Diagram

◆ Finishing

1. Choose your own quilting design. Depending on your selection, follow the directions in "Marking the Quilting Lines" on page 19 to prepare the quilt top for quilting.

2. Referring to "Layering the Quilt" on page 19, center and layer the quilt top and the batting over the backing; baste.

3. Quilt as desired (see "Quilting Techniques" on pages 20–21).

4. Trim the batting and backing even with the edges of the quilt top. Referring to "Binding" on pages 22–23, join the 2½" × 42" light blue strips to make the binding. Sew the binding to the quilt.

5. Make and attach a label to the quilt.

B
Hat
Cut 6 and 3 reversed

A
Dress
Cut 6 and 3 reversed

Embroidery detail

Dorothy's Garden Girls
Patterns and
Appliqué and Embroidery Placement Diagram

ALL THE CENTERS ARE DANCING

he hexagon flowers of this scrappy, happy quilt can barely contain their colorful centers. In fact, the flower centers have escaped! Look carefully: you might find them dancing across the quilt.

Sharon Yenter

Finished quilt size: 43" × 43"
Finished block size: 8"

Materials

42"-wide fabric

⅞ yd. light solid for appliqué background blocks

1¼ yds. green '30s print for plain blocks, setting triangles, and middle border

¾ yd. green solid for leaves, stems, and inner border

¼ yd. yellow tone-on-tone print for baskets

1⅛ yds. yellow '30s print for outer border and bias binding

⅛ yd. red solid for cherries

½ yd. *total* of assorted '30s prints for hexagons and centers

2¾ yds. fabric for backing

47" × 47" piece of batting

1 yd. fusible web (optional)

Cutting

All measurements include ¼"-wide seam allowances.

From the light solid, cut:

9 oversized squares, each 9½" × 9½", for appliqué background blocks

From the green '30s print, cut:

4 squares, each 8½" × 8½", for plain blocks

2 squares, each 12⅝" × 12⅝", for side setting triangles

2 squares, each 6⅝" × 6⅝", for corner setting triangles

4 strips, each 2½" × 42", for middle border

From the green solid, cut:

4 strips, each 1" × 42", for inner border.

1 square, 22" × 22", for bias strips

From the yellow tone-on-tone print, cut:

9 squares, each 4⅜" × 4⅜", for baskets

From the yellow '30s print, cut:

5 strips, each 2¼" × 42", for outer border

1 square, 24" × 24", for bias binding

All the Centers Are Dancing
By Sharon Yenter, 1999, Seattle, Washington
Quilted by Laurie Shifrin

◢ Making the Blocks

You'll need a total of 9 appliqué blocks for this quilt. Refer to "Basic Appliqué" starting on page 11 for general appliqué techniques. Choose the appliqué method you prefer and follow the instructions appropriate to that method.

1. Refer to "Marking and Cutting Fabric" on page 11 and use the block appliqué placement diagram below to prepare and mark the 9½" light background squares for appliqué.

2. Referring to "Making Templates" on page 11, use the patterns on page 103 to make templates. Trace the templates and cut 52 A pieces and 9 C pieces from the green solid, 8 E pieces from the red solid, and 43 B pieces and 12 D pieces from the assorted '30s prints. Add a scant ¼"-wide seam allowance around the traced lines as you cut.

3. Using your preferred appliqué method, appliqué the following pieces *in order* to each light background block: 4 A, 1 C, and 3 B. Trim the appliquéd blocks to measure 8½" × 8½".

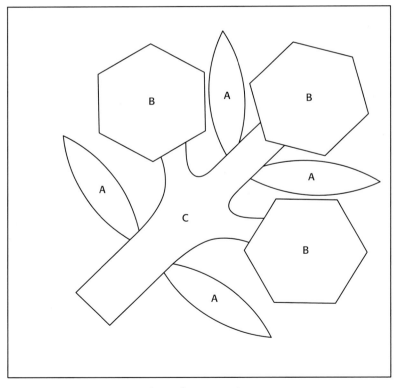

Appliqué Placement Diagram

4. With right sides together, align a 4⅜" yellow square with the bottom corner of each appliqué block. Draw a line from corner to corner as shown, and stitch directly on the line. Trim away the excess, leaving a ¼" seam allowance. Press the triangle toward the corner.

Assembling the Quilt

1. Referring to step 5 on page 8, cut each 12⅝" green print square twice diagonally to make 8 side setting triangles.

2. Referring to step 4 on page 8, cut each 6⅝" green print square in half diagonally to make 4 corner setting triangles.

3. Refer to the quilt assembly diagram below and "Making Diagonally Set Quilts" on page 17. Arrange the appliqué blocks, 8½" green print plain blocks, side setting triangles, and corner setting triangles in a pleasing and balanced color arrangement as shown.

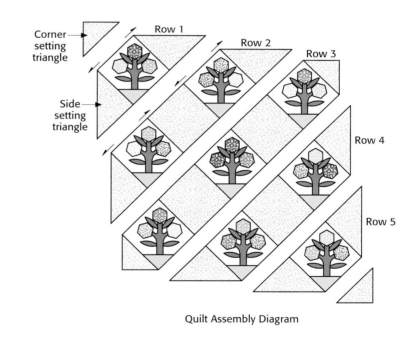

Quilt Assembly Diagram

4. Pin, then sew the blocks, squares, and setting triangles to make 5 diagonal rows as shown. Press all seams away from the appliqué blocks.

5. Carefully pin the rows together, matching the seams; then sew the rows together. Press. Add corner setting triangles to the corners to complete the quilt center.

Adding the Inner Borders

1. With right sides together and long raw edges aligned, sew a 1" × 42" green solid strip to a 2½" × 42" green print strip to make a border unit. Make 4 units. Press the seams toward the green print strip.

2. Referring to "Adding Borders" on pages 17–18, measure the quilt through its horizontal center and trim 2 border units to this measurement. Pin and sew the trimmed border units to the top and bottom edges of the quilt top. Be sure to position the green solid strip closest to the quilt center. Press the seams toward the border unit. Repeat to measure, trim, and add the remaining border units to the sides of the quilt top.

Appliquéing the Border

1. Measure and lightly mark the center point on the long edge of each side setting triangle. Using this mark as a guide, position 2 remaining A pieces (leaves) in each side setting triangle as shown. The lower tips of the leaves should measure approximately 2" from the inner border strip. Use your preferred method to appliqué the leaves in place (see "Basic Appliqué" starting on page 11). Position and appliqué an E piece (cherry) at the spot where the 2 leaves meet as shown.

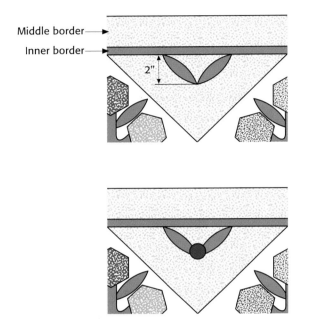

2. Use a compass or a dinner plate to lightly mark an arc over each appliquéd leaf and cherry cluster as shown. The top of the arc should measure approximately 3" from the inner border strip.

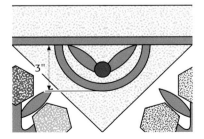

3. Referring to "Making Bias Stems for Appliqué" on pages 15–16, use the 22" square of green solid fabric to cut, sew, and press eight $\frac{1}{2}$" × 10" bias strip segments for the arcs. Pin or baste the appliqué bias strip over the arc you have marked in each side setting triangle; then appliqué the strip to the quilt top.

4. Referring to the quilt photo below for guidance, position and appliqué a remaining B hexagon over both ends of each bias strip from step 3.

5. Randomly position and appliqué the D (dancing center) pieces to the quilt. Refer to the photo on page 97 for guidance, or determine your own placement. Centers may even "dance" into the plain squares if you like.

Adding the Outer Border

1. Referring to "Adding Borders" on pages 17–18, measure the quilt through its horizontal center and trim the yellow print $2\frac{1}{4}$" × 42" outer border strips to this measurement. Pin and sew the trimmed border strips to the top and bottom edges of the quilt. Press seams toward the outer borders.

2. Cut 1 remaining $2\frac{1}{4}$" × 42" outer border strip in half. Sew these pieces to the remaining two $2\frac{1}{4}$" × 42" strips. Measure, trim, and sew the strips to the sides of the quilt. Press toward the outer borders.

Detail of quilt

◤ Finishing

1. Choose your own quilting design. Depending on your selection, follow the directions in "Marking the Quilting Lines" on page 19 to prepare the quilt top for quilting.

2. Divide the backing fabric crosswise into 2 equal panels of approximately 49" each. Remove the selvages and join the pieces to make a single large backing panel.

3. Referring to "Layering the Quilt" on page 19, center and layer the quilt top and the batting over the backing; then baste.

4. Quilt as desired (see "Quilting Techniques" on pages 20–21).

5. Trim the batting and backing even with the edges of the quilt top. Refer to the instructions for bias-grain binding on page 22 to cut 2¼"-wide bias strips from the 24" yellow '30s print square, for a total of approximately 182" of bias binding. Sew the binding strips to the quilt.

6. Make and attach a label to the quilt.

All the Centers Are Dancing
Patterns

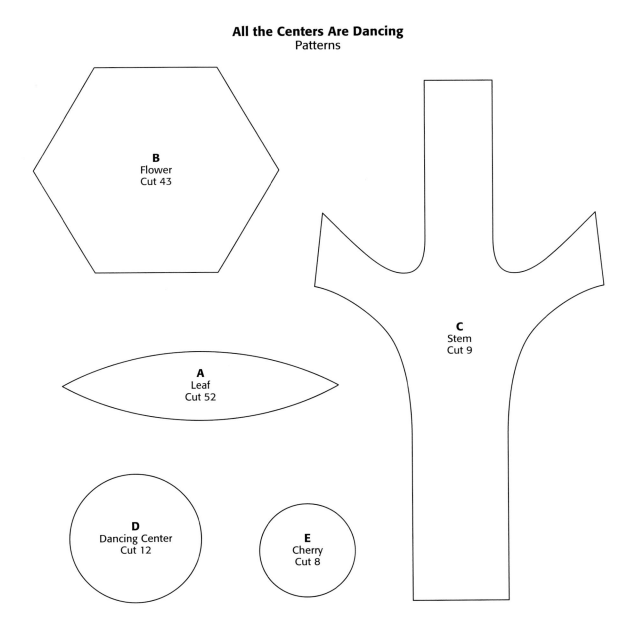

GRANDMA BUCHANAN'S PORCH

This quilt was inspired by an antique quilt pictured on page 94 of Nancy J. Martin's book, *Make Room for Quilts* (Martingale & Company, 1998). I was able to complement the '30s fabrics in my stash with a sweet, pink ticking (pinstripe) to create this charming quilt in the enduringly popular strippy style. The simple Four Patch blocks become more interesting when arranged on point. Designed as a tribute to my maternal great-great-grandmother, Katy Buchanan, who was also a quilter, this quilt evokes thoughts of summer porches, cool lemonade, and time well spent. Aptly named "Grandma Buchanan's Porch," this quilt will be an heirloom for your family, too. My friend, Judy Allen, provided the beautiful machine quilting that is also reminiscent of the '30s.

Beth Kovich

> Finished quilt size: $84\frac{5}{8}$" × $108\frac{5}{8}$"
> Finished block size: $8\frac{1}{2}$"

◤ Materials

42"-wide fabric

$2\frac{3}{8}$ yds. *total* of assorted '30s prints for blocks

$4\frac{5}{8}$ yds. white solid for blocks, sashing, and border

$3\frac{1}{2}$ yds. pink pinstripe for setting triangles and binding

$7\frac{3}{4}$ yds. for backing

88" × 112" piece of batting

◤ Cutting

All measurements include $\frac{1}{4}$"-wide seam allowances.

From the assorted '30s prints, cut:

    A total of 40 strips, each 2" × 42", for blocks

From the white solid, cut:

    40 squares, each $3\frac{1}{2}$" × $3\frac{1}{2}$", for blocks

    40 squares, each $5\frac{1}{2}$" × $5\frac{1}{2}$", for blocks

    80 strips, each 3" × 3", for blocks

    10 strips, each $3\frac{1}{2}$" × 42", for vertical sashing

    9 strips, each $6\frac{1}{2}$" × 42", for borders

From the pink pinstripe, cut:

    18 squares, each $13\frac{1}{4}$" × $13\frac{1}{4}$", for side setting triangles

    10 squares,, each 7" × 7", for corner setting triangles

    10 strips, each $2\frac{1}{2}$" × 42", for binding

Grandma Buchanan's Porch
By Beth Kovich, 1999, Woodinville, Washington
Machine quilted by Judy Allen

Making the Pieced Blocks

You'll need a total of 40 blocks for this quilt. Refer to "Machine Piecing" on pages 9–11 for general piecing techniques. Be sure to use four matching four-patch units for each block.

1. With right sides together and long raw edges aligned, sew 2 assorted 2" × 42" strips together to make a strip set. Press the seams to one side. Make 20 strip sets. Each strip set should measure 3½" × 42" when sewn and pressed.

2. Crosscut each strip set into 16 segments that are 2" wide. You will have a total of 320 segments.

Make 20 strip sets.

2"

Cut 16 segments
from each strip set
(320 total).

> ### Beth's Tip
> *The 16 segments from each strip set will be enough for 2 finished blocks. Stack segments together that are alike to make assembling the block easier.*

3. Arrange 2 matching segments as shown. Carefully matching the center seam, pin and sew the segments together to make a four-patch unit. Press the seams to one side. Make 160.

Make 160.

4. Cut the 5½" white squares twice diagonally for a total of 160 side triangles (see step 5 on page 8).

5. Cut the 3" white squares once diagonally for a total of 160 corner triangles (see step 4 on page 8).

6. Arrange 4 white corner triangles, 4 white side triangles, 4 matching four-patch units, and one 3½" white square in diagonal rows as shown. Be sure to orient the same-color squares in the four-patch units in the same direction.

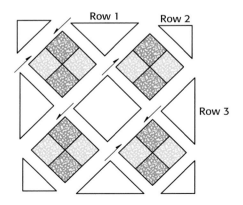

Row 1   Row 2

Row 3

7. With right sides together, pin and sew the units together into diagonal rows. Press the seams toward the four-patch units. Carefully pin the rows together, matching the seams. Sew the rows together. Press the seams to one side. Sew a corner triangle to each corner to complete a block. Make 40.

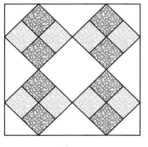

Make 40.

◆ Assembling the Quilt Top

1. Cut the $13\frac{1}{4}$" pink squares twice diagonally for a total of 72 side setting triangles. You will only use 70.
2. Cut the 7" pink squares once diagonally for a total of 20 corner setting triangles.

3. Refer to the quilt assembly diagram on page 108 and the color photo on page 105 to arrange 8 blocks and 14 side setting triangles into diagonal rows. Pin and sew the blocks and triangles together into diagonal rows. Press the seams toward the pink side setting triangles.

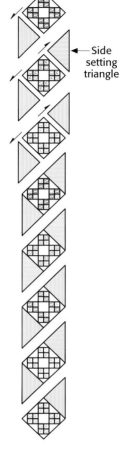

← Side setting triangle

4. Pin and sew the diagonal rows together to make one long vertical row. Press the seams to one side. Sew a corner setting triangle to each corner to complete the vertical row. Make 5.

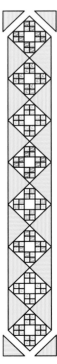

Make 5.

5. Sew the remaining 3½" × 42" white sashing strips end to end to make one long continuous strip. Cut the strip into four 3½" × 100" strips for the vertical sashing. These are cut a little longer than necessary and will be trimmed in the next step.

6. Alternate the vertical rows of blocks and white sashing strips, beginning and ending with a row of blocks as shown in the quilt assembly diagram. Aligning the tops of the rows, pin and sew the rows together. Press the seams toward the white sashing strips. Trim the excess sashing strips even with the rows of blocks.

Trim excess sashing strips.

Quilt Assembly Diagram

7. Sew the 6½" × 42" white strips end to end to make one long continuous strip. Cut the strip into two 6½" × 96¾" strips for the side borders, and two 6½" × 84⅝" strips for the top and bottom borders.

8. Pin and sew the 6½" × 96¾" strips to the sides of the quilt. Press the seams toward the border strips. Repeat to sew the 6½" × 84⅝" strips to the top and bottom edges of the quilt.

Finishing

1. Choose your own quilting design. Depending on your selection, follow the directions in "Marking the Quilting Lines" on page 19 to prepare the quilt top for quilting.

2. Divide the backing fabric crosswise into 3 equal panels of approximately 92" each. Remove the selvages and join the pieces to make a single large backing panel.

3. Referring to "Layering the Quilt" on page 19, center and layer the quilt top and the batting over the backing; baste.

4. Quilt as desired (see "Quilting Techniques" on pages 20–21).

5. Trim the batting and backing even with the edges of the quilt top. Referring to "Binding" on pages 22–23, use the $2\frac{1}{2}$" × 42" strips to make the binding. Sew the binding to the quilt.

6. Make and attach a label to the finished quilt.

ABOUT THE CONTRIBUTORS

◤ Sandy Bonsib

Sandy Bonsib made her first quilt in the early 1970's. Since then, she has become a well-respected quiltmaking teacher. She says, "For me, this is the best of both worlds, since teaching is my profession and quilting is my passion." Sandy is the author of *Quilting Your Memories: Inspiration for Designing with Image Transfers* and *Folk Art Quilts: A Fresh Look*. Sandy lectures and teaches for quilt guilds and conferences around the country. She lives in Issaquah, Washington, with her husband, their two teenage children, and many animals.

◤ Mimi Dietrich

Mimi Dietrich lives with her husband and two sons in Baltimore, Maryland. She is a member of the Baltimore Heritage Quilters Guild and is a "founding mother" of the Village Quilters in Catonsville, Maryland, and the Baltimore Appliqué Society. She quilts on Monday nights with Monday Night Madness and on Fridays with The Catonsville Quilt and Tea Society. Mimi is the author of several bestselling books, including *Happy Endings*, *Baltimore Bouquets*, and *The Easy Art of Appliqué* (with Roxi Eppler). When she is not appliquéing, Mimi is teaching appliqué classes!

◤ Carol Doak

Carol Doak is a bestselling author, popular teacher, and award-winning quiltmaker. Her teaching career has taken her to many cities in the United States and beyond. Her lighthearted approach and ability to teach beginners as well as advanced quilters have earned her high marks from workshop participants wherever she travels.

Several books have included Carol's blue-ribbon quilts. Carol has been featured in several national quilt magazines, and her quilts have appeared on the covers of *Quilter's Newsletter Magazine*, *Quilt World*, *Quilting Today*, *Lady's Circle Patchwork Quilts*, and *McCall's Quilting*.

Carol's bestselling books, approaching half a million in print, include *Easy Machine Paper Piecing*, *Show Me How to Paper Piece*, *Easy Stash Quilts*, *Easy Paper-Pieced Miniature Quilts*, and *Your First Quilt Book (or it should be!)*.

Carol lives in Windham, New Hampshire, where she claims the cold winters give her plenty of reason to stockpile a fabric stash for insulation!

◤ Joan Whitelaw Hanson

Joan Whitelaw Hanson's infatuation with fabric began at an early age as she spent